waterside living

waterside living

inspirational homes by lakes, rivers and the sea

Leslie Geddes-Brown

photography by **Jan Baldwin**

RYLAND
PETERS
& SMALL

LONDON NEW YORK

Senior designer **Louise Leffler**
Senior editor **Henrietta Heald**
Location research manager **Kate Brunt**
Location research **Sarah Hepworth**
Production **Patricia Harrington**
Art director **Gabriella Le Grazie**
Publishing director **Alison Starling**

Stylist **Sylvie Jones**
Proofreader and indexer **Laura Hicks**

First published in the United Kingdom in 2001
by Ryland Peters & Small
Kirkman House
12–14 Whitfield Street
London W1T 2RP
www.rylandpeters.com
10 9 8 7 6 5 4 3 2 1

Text © Leslie Geddes-Brown 2001
Design and photographs © Ryland Peters & Small 2001

The author's moral rights have been asserted.

ISBN 1 84172 170 0

Jacket picture credits
Front Elena Colombo's cottage on the east end of Long Island.
Back Top row: l Camp Kent designed by Alexandra Champalimaud; **r** Roderick
& Gillie Jameses' house in Devon designed by Roderick James Architects and
built by Carpenter Oak & Woodland Co. Ltd. **Bottom row: l** Interior Designer
Philip Hooper's own house in East Sussex; **c** Elena Colombo's cottage on the
east end of Long Island; **r** Compound by a lakeside in the mountains of Western
Maine designed by Stephen Blatt Architects.

A CIP record for this book is available from
the British Library.

Printed and bound in China.

contents

introduction

I feel well qualified to write about waterside living. For the past eight years I have lived in a house surrounded by a moat that, at its widest, is 15 metres (nearly 50 ft) from bank to bank. Two sides of the house, which dates from 1380, rise directly from the water. Eric Sandon, writing about the old houses of Suffolk, describes it as having 'the look of a vessel at anchor'.

So I do know about the pleasures of living with the ripples lapping directly outside my dining room, reflected on my kitchen ceiling, and the ducks, coots and moorhens cruising past the open window where we sit on summer evenings. We can see our group of golden orfe – fish now well over 30 cm (1 ft) long – swimming barely below the surface and, gliding just above the surface, the swallows, house martins and swifts that visit us from Africa every summer. They love the water, which attracts the flies. It also attracts dragonflies resembling small helicopters and water voles that busy themselves along the banks. When we moved in there was also the bright turquoise flash of a kingfisher, which left when we had to dredge the moat. Recently we have put in some sacrificial fish in the hope of attracting it back.

Living by water in summer is not only beautiful but full of incident. The mallards have tiny ducklings, the dabchick arrives with his mate and teaches his babies to dive as best he can, and the coots fight enormous territorial battles punctuated by sharp clicks from wide-open beaks. Sitting beside our window, with a large decoy swan made by the brilliant Guy Taplin, we are blissfully cool even on the hottest of days.

I also know something of the problems of waterside living since I was brought up in the low-lying city of York in the north of England. My father was a doctor there and, at least once, had to visit his sick patients by horse and cart or, if they were nearer the River Ouse, by rowing boat. We daily lived with the risk that we, too, would be flooded – it never happened because our house was on a main road 200 metres (650 ft) from the river, but we became attuned to the regular alarms. Fed by numerous tributaries in the Yorkshire dales, the Ouse was a dangerous flow, regularly sweeping away young men who dived in after a night at one of the waterside pubs.

Yet, even with the risk of flooding – or, as cliffside houseowners discover, the risk of having your windows regularly blown out by gales – once you have discovered the delights of waterside living, you never want to go away again. The attraction is the constant change, as I found out when staying at Brantwood, the house of the Victorian art critic John Ruskin, which overlooks Coniston Water in the Lake District. Every day, every hour, every minute brought variations in the clouds, the atmosphere and the light that played over the lake and the crag known as the Old Man of Coniston, which brooded over the water on the opposite shore. I have therefore been delighted to discover that the owners of the houses featured here have found pleasures from their waterside existence as equally diverse as those I get from mine. We all, it seems, have something different to enjoy.

the essence of

waterside living

It must have been early in the history of civilization when water – lakes, beaches, cliffs, rivers, harbours, lakes, moats and pools – changed from being simply a security feature to being a source of pure pleasure.

According to legend, Venice was founded on 25 March 421, at midday exactly. It was a Friday. No doubt the original colonizers sought out the lagoon with its hundreds of tiny islands as a place of safety. It was hard for raiders to find their way around the marshes and inlets, which the residents knew by heart. But then, security is extremely comforting, and the Venetians soon began to adore their damp bog of a hideaway. Even today, years after the decline of 'La Serenissima', we can see how they gave their city presents of jewels and statues, and carved wellheads and built houses so ornate that they look like iced cakes rising straight from the murky canals. These, in turn, attracted artists who were enchanted by the light which comes from the combination of water, marble and sun, and who, to this day, make Venice the most painted city in the world. It is also among the most

visited cities and one perfectly attuned to romance. On my first visit I came across an exotic dark-haired woman walking a cheetah on a jewelled lead. This, to me, has summed up its sinister attractions.

It was the desire for security that made people dig moats around their houses – but how the water enhances the buildings. Look at the Loire chateaux with their stone walls rising from still sheets of water. Look at the vernacular buildings of England that are moated and full of charm. My area of Suffolk has more moats than any other part of Britain – at least 568, of which about 200 are linked with ancient halls. Even the word 'moat' comes from Middle English and dates from around 1150. Moats were partly defensive, and also handy for watering cattle and keeping fish, but historians speculate that they were fashionable in Suffolk in the 15th and 16th centuries – the equivalent of owning an indoor swimming pool today.

Castles were also moated against marauders (cattle thieves and bands of brigands rather than armies) or perched on cliffs and plugs of rock directly

THIS PAGE AND OPPOSITE
To live by the sea is like being always on holiday, whether you spend hours walking on the sands or enjoy fighting a gale in front of the comfort of a driftwood fire. Owners find the urge to decorate with seagoing impedimenta virtually irresistible: hurricane lamps, lifebelts, deck chairs and fancy verandahs are elements of a constant theme. Then there's the entertaining – friends can't be kept at bay, and you need bowls full of sensuous food to satisfy appetites stoked by that famous sea air.

above the sea, or on peninsulas in Scottish lochs. Even as late as the 1745 rebellion of Bonnie Prince Charlie, life was uncertain in Britain and worse in the rest of Europe. But these rocky strongholds often had great presence. Once you've seen the island of Mont-St-Michel, off France's north-west coast, and its Cornish twin, St Michael's Mount, you will never forget their powerful silhouettes.

Before I had my own waterside retreat, the place where I most wanted to live was Lindisfarne Castle on Holy Island, off England's north-east coast, converted into a house by Sir Edwin Lutyens at the start of the 20th century. It was the combination of the wild Northumbrian seas that lash this historic island, with its past of Viking raids, and the comfort that Lutyens had built into the interior through massive stone walls, narrow windows and great welcoming fires that seemed irresistibly attractive. Abbeys, too, have been built beside water, and the natural rivers and streams were artificially widened to form fish ponds and watercress beds, pools for watering

the animals and others to irrigate the soil. The Cistercians were unrivalled at picking wonderful sites. Bolton Abbey rises from the valley of the River Wharfe, Rievaulx Abbey from the River Rye, and the majestic Fountains Abbey sprawls peacefully in the valley of the River Nidd – all of them in Yorkshire.

Waterside living often has an element of danger about it – the lash of storms that make landfall on your cliffs, the driving rain and howling winds that keen around the house, the risk of flooding and drowning. On a dark winter's night, as the gales intensify, I wouldn't be anywhere other than in my moat room in front of a log fire big enough to take tree trunks or in the four-poster bed upstairs in a room which jetties out over the water so I can see its white horses through the floor beneath my feet.

The ancient Egyptians were civilized enough to create ornamental water features in their gardens some 4000 years ago as did the Moors in Spain as long ago as AD 900. Both the

Taj Mahal, with its canals reflecting the white-marble building, and the Palace of Versailles, with its spurting fountains and curvaceous ponds, were created then. There was no added spice of danger in these elegant watery gardens – they were built for grandeur and the contemplation of manmade beauty.

Gradually, as security became less important, the adventurous and the rich went in search of water in all its dramatic forms. The Grand Tour, all the rage in the 18th century – though the first tourists actually started going to Italy during the late 17th century – saw rich young gentlemen from northern Europe travel to the Classical lands in search of excitement, education and booty. Their adventures took them down the Rhine, sampling the hock and not liking it much, and admiring the craggy, impregnable castles that the robber barons built to take tolls from the travellers who crossed Germany by boat. 'Let those who delight in picturesque country repair to the borders of the Rhine and follow the road we took,' wrote the Grand Tourist

Why are so many coastal buildings brightly painted and small-scale? From harbours such as Tobermory on the Scottish island of Mull to the beach huts of Essex in south-eastern England, from the colourful weatherboarded shacks found on the eastern seaboard of the USA to the rainbow terraces of San Francisco, the urge is there. These colourful scenes come from Dangar Island, near Sydney, where a white boat fronts a group of simple, unadorned boatsheds in pale yellows, blues and white. The answer may be that people faced with gales, storms and the constant danger of the sea like to have cosy, small buildings around them for comfort.

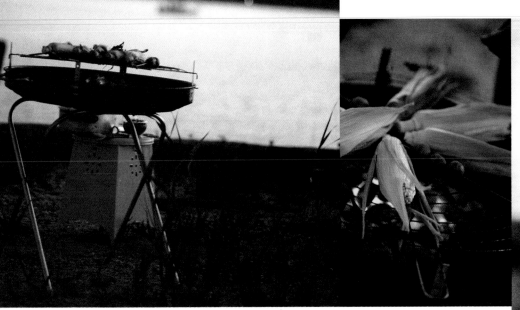

WE YEARN FOR THE NATURAL SEAWASHED PEBBLE RATHER THAN THE HEWN BLOCK OF STONE. WE HAVE REDISCOVERED THE MAGIC PATTERNS OF SEASHELLS AND CORAL. WE LONG FOR MOONLIGHT ON WATER AND SUNLIGHT RIPPLING ON THE CEILING.

William Beckford in 1780. 'In some places it is suspended like a cornice, above the waters, in others it winds between lofty steeps and broken acclivities, shaded by woods and and clothed with an endless variety of plants and flowers.'

The tourists arrived in Italy via the Alps with their snow-covered peaks and still mountain lakes, or took the easy way – a boat to Genoa. Then they would progress through Italy admiring the scenery – the Arno bisecting Florence, the Tiber winding through the ruins of Rome, the lakes of Como and Garda – before reaching Naples. 'See Naples and die' summed up the romantic views on offer there. There was Vesuvius, erupting throughout the 18th and 19th centuries; Pompeii and Herculaneum, which had recently been uncovered from volcanic debris; the wonderful villas along the Bay of Naples itself; and the Aeolian islands and Sicily. Grand tourists swarmed to Sicily to see the Greek temples of Paestum. They visited the island of

THIS PAGE AND OPPOSITE
The 20th century was the era of holidays on the beach, and by the end of it the world had elevated the joys and pleasures of beach living to a fine art. The USA inspired the seashore barbecue (invented by Spanish fishermen who arrived as pioneers). Elena Colombo, whose deliberately **junk-style cabin sits on a Long Island beach, has created her own piece of perfection in the relaxed meal cooked over embers on a balmy summer evening. Essential ingredients include seafood and sweetcorn, gently scented smoke, startling sunsets – and a group of contented friends.**

Capri, where the Emperor Tiberius had earlier discovered his own enjoyment of waterside living, and they admired the volcanoes of Etna and Stromboli.

The French artist Madame Vigée-Lebrun was ecstatic about the captivating view from her own house in Naples. 'On Sunday, young peasants in their best clothes danced the tarantella in front of my house, beating a little drum, and every evening I could see fishermen, the flames from their torches reflected in the sea.'

Sometimes the smells from an itinerant kitchen using stale cooking oil below her windows forced her to look at the view through gaps in the closed shutters. 'But how beautiful it is, the sea at Naples. Often I spent whole hours watching it during the night, when the waves were calm, silvery in the splendid moonlight. Often, too, I used to take a boat for an excursion and enjoy the magnificent spectacle presented by this city which one always sees in its entirety, like some amphitheatre.'

Along with the milordi came quantities of artists from France and England, eager to capture the seascapes of the cities along with the torrents which crashed down the slopes of the Alps and the famous lakes and the resorts beside them. One such was Thomas Jones, whose quiet watercolours evoke perfectly the lakes of Albano and Nemi and, naturally, the Bay of Naples too. His diary records in 1780, 'Scrambled up the rocks and thro' the woods and vineyards until we got to the summits of the mountains so as to command a view of both bays at the same time. Among these woods, hills and vineyards are interspersed many beautiful neat little villas, most delightfully situated.'

Artists such as Thomas Jones, Francis Towne and Alexander Cozens captured the picturesque but controlled wilderness of Italy which, in turn, led to the 19th-century craze for the Romantic in Britain. If the rich could make the trek to the Mediterranean, the middle classes could take their coaches – and, later, the train – up to the Lake District, the Black Mountains of Wales and the Highlands of Scotland. Intrepid Victorian ladies visited the Alps and climbed the Matterhorn in their crinolines, while Queen Victoria herself took a boat down the Rhine.

This was the era when poets flocked to Windermere and Ullswater to be inspired by the lowering mountains and the dark lakes beneath; when Victorian painters travelled over the borders to capture Betws-y-Coed and Snowdon as the bracken turned amber, and put up easels on Scottish hillsides to picture the deer drinking at the side of Loch Lomond or mysterious Loch Ness.

Queen Victoria, seduced by the romance of the Highlands, decreed that Balmoral should be built for her summer holidays – and established a tradition that has been kept up by the British Royal Family ever since. Encouraged by Victoria's enthusiasm for all things Scottish, rich industrialists rented fishing lodges beside the great

trout and salmon rivers of the Spey and Dee or flocked to the islands. Arran became a resort and the Duke of Buccleuch built a castle on Bute.

Islands have remained romantic ever since. Two members of my husband's family have actually owned islands. One, Vulcano, is a small volcanic blob among the larger Aeolian islands off Sicily. Named after Vulcan, the god of fire and blacksmiths, it consists of two volcanic cones, one dead and the other dormant, below which are warm springs and stinking sulphur baths. Italians – and the pop star Madonna – still flock to Vulcano to immerse themselves in this warm mud, so in its way this island is a proper resort. It is a strange and eerie place with its lingering bad-egg smell, its black beaches and weird lava rocks that rear up from the sea. Even the wild flowers are exotic.

My husband's ancestor lived on the island in the 1880s and was regularly visited by his relations, who were cruising the Mediterranean by steam yacht – but it all ended in tears when the volcano erupted, covering the gardens and vineyards in volcanic ash several metres deep.

The second island was Eigg, 16 km (10 miles) out from the tiny port of Arisaig on the west coast of Scotland, which can still be reached only by boat. His parents spent their honeymoon there, in a kind of Mediterranean villa surrounded by palm trees, courtesy of the Gulf Stream, which keeps the

THIS PAGE AND OPPOSITE Tropical beaches framed by palms are the stuff of most people's fantasy holidays. White squeaky sand, pelicans and hummingbirds, conch shells and coconuts enlivened with rum punch are what we dream about. These evocative scenes are all from Barbados, from the man skilfully climbing a slender tree trunk to pick coconuts (falling coconuts are a major hazard in the Caribbean) to the weird way bananas defy logic and grow upside down. The strange ridged trunks are of palm, banana and bamboo.

climate mild. It was a place of refuge for all the family. One, a famous writer, regularly retired there to complete his books. Islands offer this kind of isolation to those who need to relax and those who need to work. Complete in themselves, they keep the stresses and strains of the world at bay.

I myself have had a long love affair with islands. However small they are, they seem complete. On the tiny island of Pantelleria, once a prison for Italian fascists, I met my first olive trees while I was scrambling down the cliffs to the sea. A young *carabiniere*, in his smart uniform, climbed up and picked me a branch, complete with infant olives. On the beach the fishermen cooked their own sardines with a touch of local olive oil on portable barbecues. On Ischia I visited the composer Sir William Walton, whose wife has created extraordinary gardens around their cliffside villa, and on Elba I saw the little villa where Napoleon spent his first years of captivity.

Tobago, a tiny island in the West Indies almost completely devoted to pleasure, allowed me to lie on its soft white beaches with whispering palm trees looking impossibly like a tourist poster. Tuna lurked under wooden piers, waiting to be caught and grilled for lunch. During breakfast by the beach, minute hummingbirds would come to suck sweetness from the tropical flowers. And I've always had a soft spot for the Bahamas, where my luggage once went without me, to return to England with a label that read 'Welcome to the Bahamas'. Later visits proved my luggage had had a wonderful time.

I've taken ferries to the islands of Mull and Iona on stormy days and been delighted to arrive safely; I've bought pieces of furniture on Anglesey and Arran – a very stupid idea since they have to be shipped to their destination at vast expense. A favourite hotel at the end of the Crinan Canal on the west coast of Scotland has given

me unrivalled views of Jura and its hills over the darkening water of a famous whirlpool, and I crossed the sea to Skye before they built the bridge and spoilt it for ever.

If the 19th century was the time of islands and romantic lakes, the 20th was the time when beaches and swimming were invented. The travel writer Eric Newby describes the palatial hotels that were built all along the Riviera from 1912 onwards. They were designed 'for the reception of royalty, which included whole squads of grand dukes (sightings of a dozen at a time were not uncommon; they used to come for the weekend from St Petersburg in special trains), noblemen, statesmen and millionaires'. They came 'to play at the casinos and be given the kiss of life by such grandes horizontales as La Belle Otero, Gaby Deslys and Liane de Pouget'. The Victorians may have stripped off in little wheeled carts dragged by donkeys into the sea, but it was not until the time of Coco Chanel that it

was smart to lounge in chic palazzo pyjamas on the Riviera. King Edward VIII went on a scandalous cruise with Mrs Simpson, and the Carlton Hotel in Cannes suggested to the Aga Khan that they should bottle his bath water and sell it to the faithful. The tiny coastal village of Portofino was all the rage with 1950s Hollywood stars such as Rex Harrison and Errol Flynn, who misbehaved at the Hotel Splendido, and, shortly after, Brigitte Bardot turned an unpopular fishing village called St Tropez into a resort that still attracts the rich and famous. Sun tans were *de rigueur*, bikinis were essential, and seaside hedonism was the envy of all those who could not afford the outrageous prices.

After the First World War, Gerald and Sara Murphy – two wealthy Americans transformed by F. Scott Fitzgerald into characters in his novel *Tender is the Night* – discovered La Garoupe while staying with Cole Porter at Cap d'Antibes. No one went to the Riviera in the

summer then or bathed in the sea. Gerald Murphy wrote, 'We dug out a corner of the beach and bathed there and sat in the sun, and we decided that this was where we wanted to be.' They had invented a whole new way of life – one which attracted Picasso, writers such as Somerset Maugham, Ernest Hemingway and Françoise Sagan, and film directors such as Roger Vadim – which was to last until travel and the beautiful life became the property of ordinary tourists and, therefore, less worth having.

The modernist architects of the 20th century – Le Corbusier, Frank Lloyd Wright and the Bauhaus group – created a style that was perfect for the waterside. Because it was now possible to make plate glass in enormous sheets, and because central heating and air conditioning were becoming standard, houses could embrace hugely dramatic views. They could be given glass walls from floor to ceiling, and overhanging balconies and verandahs to make good views even more spectacular. One house I know in Devon, created at the very end of the 20th century, has full-length windows that can be electrically lowered into the basement, leaving the main living room open to the sunlight and views over the sea beyond. Butterflies flutter into the open space and sea breezes waft the curtains.

Though these dramatically open, flat-roofed houses stormed over California, with its miles of wonderful Pacific cliffs and beaches, they proved less attractive on the east coast of America, where the

WASP bankers and politicians began to colonize the Hamptons, Martha's Vineyard and Long Island. Holiday homes here were strictly vernacular: weatherboarded, sash-windowed and, towards the end of the 20th century, full of American country antiques and found objects. Martha Stewart was the queen of this movement, just as Parish Hadley had created American versions of the English country look two decades earlier.

Curiously, as the 20th century moved on, the west coast's love of waterside modernism grew more exotic and tropical, while the east coast's style and that of England have merged. So there is Ralph Lauren in New York celebrating very English classic clothes in very English gardens, while in England waterside houses espouse Shaker styles and American duck decoys. We have adopted many of Nancy Lancaster's formidably foresighted ideas in English country houses, while modern-day stars like Tommy Hilfiger have hired Colefax and Fowler.

At the other side of the world, Australia is turning its back on British influences in favour of the Bauhaus and Lloyd Wright Cubist approach. Currently this is one of the most innovatively artistic countries in the world, and that goes for architecture as much as literature and gardening. And the country has some of the most beautiful and wild settings on offer. How many of us can enjoy the luxury of living on an island without any roads yet go to work each day in a city as vibrant as Sydney?

Fashions come and go – look what has happened to sun tans – but great cities like Stockholm, San Francisco and Sydney have always been built at strategic points. There are few that are not built on rivers, around safe harbours or at important ocean-crossing points. Just as the Scottish islands were less remote 200 years ago than they are now, because all traffic was waterborne, the people who sited cities in history were well aware that water was the source of life. Iron Age forts and besieged castles could hold out on hills for a short time but, without water, impregnability was dangerous.

Many of the town houses most in demand are still those with river views. If you can look out over the Seine or the Hudson, the Mississippi or the Thames, the Rhine or the Arno, you will have paid a premium for your position. Similarly, those who can see the harbour and sea around San Francisco or the world-famous opera house and bridge in Sydney can reckon that they own some of the most famous vistas the world can offer.

Stockholm, like Venice, seems all about water, though in Stockholm the light is cooler and more steely. Its colourful houses – like those of Tobermory on the Scottish island of Mull – are reflected in the waters of the harbour, and the fish market is a foodie's dream. From Stockholm the Swedes take boats to other islands for long, lazy summer holidays. In their short sunny season they have perfected the art of waterside living, with small, familiar boathouses and summer houses built directly on the water, each with windows opening onto the perfect view. Interiors are left simple and friendly, with only the softest watery colours on walls and furniture.

I believe that increasing numbers of people will take to the waterside in the 21st century, as the Swedes and the Americans have always done, even though scientists think that global warming makes rivers and seas increasingly dangerous. Just as the 18th century was the period of the Grand Tour and the 19th century that of romantic nature, just as the 20th century

RIGHT **The owner of this house is lucky enough to be able to look down on his collection of boats, used by all the family for sailing and rowing around the creeks of south Devon.**

OPPOSITE PAGE **Other owners become addicted to watching their local birdlife – from brilliantly coloured parakeets and skeins of honking wild geese to tropical pelicans which throw themselves into the water like flying Gladstone bags. It is not only humans who get a buzz from being beside water – many of the property owners have dogs and are constantly amused by their enthusiasm for diving, swimming and, rather less amusingly, nosing around among smelly dead fish.**

fully embraced the American vision of beach, pool and surf as the ideal playground, the 21st century will be an era of looking back to a nature that was pure and unsullied by man.

We yearn for the natural sea-washed pebble rather than the hewn block of stone; we have rediscovered the magic of the patterns of seashells and coral, which were last admired in the 16th century. We have turned our backs on electric light in favour of candles – at least when convenient – and we long for moonlight on water and reflected sunlight rippling on the ceiling. Where we can, we find homes unaffected by artificial light at night, places where we can see the stars and hear the seabirds as they nest on the cliffs.

As we have found, water is an elemental force. Try to harness it and it evades you; try to force it to your will and it defeats you. In a synthetic world, water is still the great force of nature. Yes, it's dangerous. Yes, it's unpredictable. And yes, it's untameable too. That is, of course, why we value it so much.

lakeside living

No continent can boast of the grandeur of its lakes with more confidence than North America, where the Great Lakes have the quality of inland seas, and even smaller lakes would engulf whole countries in Europe. These lakes have also generated their own culture, a distinctively American one that owes much to the American Indians, along with the early pioneers, the fishermen and the trappers who made a living from the wilderness.

It is the American Indians' canoes and kayaks, their methods of fishing through the ice, their artefacts and artworks that evoke lake living as it is today, while the trappers' simple log cabins and woodburning stoves, their handmade furniture and wooden decoy birds have been the inspiration for today's cabin chic. All the lake dwellers featured here are American, and all live on the edge of the lakes of the north-eastern USA, where the severity of the winters separated the men from the boys.

Fern Mallis has her weekend hideaway in the celebrated Hamptons – but, rather being than on the beach, her home overlooks a freshwater lake. Nonetheless, it has the sharp, clear light and brilliant sunsets that once attracted painters such as Jackson Pollock and William de Kooning. This is her retreat from Manhattan, a place where she has the opportunity to get

back to nature, buy vegetables fresh from the farm and sleep late. For these reasons the house is simply furnished, with a strong country feel.

For 30 years Melba and Paul Chodosh spent holidays in an early 20th-century cabin beside a lake in Maine before, with an architect's help, they converted it into a more substantial home. They spent their honeymoon there and now – with a proper kitchen at last – it is the place where they welcome their five children and their partners and up to 13 grandchildren and step-grandchildren. If ever there were a family house, this is it.

Camp Kent was exactly that – a camp on the shores of a Vermont lake – when Alexandra Champalimaud and her husband, Bruce, took it on with a group of friends. They bought it as virtually pure wilderness and fight hard to stop anything changing that. Although Alexandra is an interior decorator, their home's atmosphere has been carefully preserved.

A lakeside cabin in Maine's south-western mountains was struck by lightning and destroyed within months of the present owner, Lynn, finding it. Nothing daunted, Lynn built a new home, which she used first as a weekend retreat but which is now her main house (with winters in California). The architect Stephen Blatt won two awards for this skilful evocation of the past.

LEFT **A jetty and a boat ready for adventure invite the owner and her guests to step down towards the water. As well as the house and garden, the shore is frequently an integral part of waterside life.**

RIGHT **Shallow steps lead up from the decked jetty to Fern Mallis's Hampton house. but her waterside is in fact a lake rather than the sea. The shallowness of the steps makes the invitation for a morning stroll more evident.**

Hard though it may be to believe today, there was a time when nobody had heard of the Hamptons. Instead of being thronged with the beautiful people weekending their cares away after a stint in New York, the area was covered by potato fields stretching as far as the eye could see. The writer Truman Capote called it 'Kansas with a sea breeze' – and he wasn't being flattering. Perhaps that was before the idea of detox for body and soul became fashionable – before the rich and stressed gave themselves a dose of medicine in the form of a weekend of picnicking, sailing and strolling by the sea. Today the area is very different.

Fern Mallis, the current executive director of the Council of Fashion Designers of America, wanted her own slice of the Hamptons and its famous breezes – but she turned her back on the ocean and found a site on a freshwater lake. 'Every estate agent will tell you about this farmer or that one who'll never sell his fields, he's had them for 150 years. The next thing you know, you look out of the kitchen window and there are 18 houses going up. But you can't build on a lake.'

Despite the demand for building plots, this is still agricultural land. 'There are farms all over the place, growing corn, tomatoes, potatoes, squash, pumpkins and seasonal vegetables. This keeps you focused on the changing seasons. The earth is very fertile on the "east end" and everything grows, from pine trees to every conceivable flowering plant.'

No one could say the same for New York City, which is why Fern values her Hampton house. 'This is all very nourishing and important when you work and

a hedonist's hideaway

This charming shingled cottage beside a freshwater lake is the realization of a potent fantasy, redolent of the atmosphere that we are all trying to create in our homes, whether for the weekend or for everyday living.

THIS PAGE **Life by the lake consists of far more than just a glimpse of water from the windows. The décor around the rooms and windows should evoke what is outside: an old Chinese lantern, a boat-shaped dish filled with bright green apples and pears and a colourful cushion all have this effect. Meanwhile, a corner of the living area uses the simplest monochromes and rattan furniture to draw attention to the windows and their view beyond. Even the rug and the stained floor are kept as plain as can be.**

OPPOSITE PAGE **The same open-plan area also includes a series of unmatched rattan and wooden chairs around the dining table, with a line of votive candles ready to light as dusk approaches.**

live Monday to Friday in a city like New York, with concrete towers and people hustling and bustling all over the place. This house and its location keep me grounded and in touch with nature and the elements that one can easily forget in the big city.'

During these working weeks Fern Mallis will habitually go to three parties a night, four nights in a row. So weekends by the water, with not a concrete tower or a cocktail bar in sight, are an essential tool of the job – even though she can't quite bring herself to turn off the fax machine as well as the phone.

Like many other people who have bought waterside homes, Fern Mallis's love affair started long

ago. She bought the charming shingled cottage in 1996, but only after staying for several summers on the shores of the same lake, where her friend Stan Herman, the president of the Council of Fashion Designers, had long had a house. Herman is now a former head of the lake owners' association and an expert on its history. Indeed, before buying her own cottage, she helped him to transform his house, which she jokingly calls 'Villa Chintz'.

Fern acted throughout as her own architect, designer, decorator and general contractor in what the glossy magazines have called a 'white tornado' transformation. Some help came from her sister

'I decorated it in the way I did because the house itself has
a certain spirit and attitude. This is clearly a country house,
with shingles and window panes and wood floors and moulding.'

Fern Mallis has cleverly stuck to pure white for both walls and paintwork. A white-painted cupboard full of white crockery is placed between door and window in the dining area. Below is the kitchen, fitted into a corner of the main living area. All the colour comes from the bright vegetables and flowers – chosen for their freshness and local availability – along with brightly striped cushions made from folded fabrics. Similar striped pieces turn up on the jetty, also in cushion form, while zebra-striped and checked bowls offset colourful fruits.

Stephanie and Stephanie's boyfriend, Scott Bromley – both architects – but the house is essentially Fern's creation in every sense. You can tell why she's a top executive from her reaction to the work, which would have had most of us staring at a blank wall with towels over our heads in exhaustion. 'I removed several walls and opened up the space to the extraordinary views of the lake from all windows. I had to replace many windows, lay tile flooring and completely gut the kitchen and install a new one – all of which is open and user-friendly, as all weekend houses are about eating, entertaining and making it all accessible. It was so exciting. Sometimes I think about finding another house and doing it all again.'

She began to plan the transformation even before the ink on the contract was dry. 'I'd decorated the house ten times in my head already.' She started by removing a lot of wood panelling, which had made the rooms very dark, and painted the rooms white instead. The views towards the lake were carefully opened up, and the kitchen became part of the main downstairs room.

One of the main attractions of the lakeside and the Hamptons is the quality of the light, which Fern has tried hard to introduce into the house. 'The Hamptons is a very special place. It is both country and beach community at the same time. The natural "east end" light is unique to the area, and the reason why painters have traditionally worked and lived there – de Kooning, Jackson Pollock, Eric Fischl, Ross Bleckner and many more.

'The light is very clear and focused. The sunsets are brilliant. The air is clean and clear without pollution. One can smell and hear the ocean, and the beaches are some of the widest and longest and most beautiful on the east coast.' However, although nature is very important to the stressed New Yorker, it should not be allowed to take over entirely. 'I love the fruit and vegetable stands. What's even better is that you can get your fresh tomatoes at the farm stand then go to the general store for your buffalo mozzarella.'

The cottage itself dictated the style that Fern Mallis created. 'I decorated it as it is because the house has a certain spirit and attitude. While I generally prefer more hard-edged modern interiors, this is clearly a country house, with shingles and window panes and wood floors and moulding.' Nonetheless, the rooms give a monochromatic feeling throughout, probably as a result of the stark white of the walls and the preponderance of huge windows,

their frames also painted white, shaded with Venetian blinds. Elsewhere she has created an informal atmosphere by refusing to make everything match. There are strongly shaped modernist chairs teamed with deep comfy sofas, both upholstered in white; dining-room chairs can be wickerwork with arms, country wooden chairs with hard seats and white cushions, or wooden armchairs with drop-in white seats. They cluster around a heavy wooden farm table which has charming and casual baskets and sisal holders full of local gourds, herbs and arrays of votive candles for the evening.

Upstairs, where Fern claims the decorative style is 'English/British/Moroccan', is what is to me a typically American half-tester bed in dark wood with heavily turned poles. This is the owner's bedroom, with extra-fine views over the freshwater lake. It has a tiny verandah and, because it is placed at the corner of the house, views over two different stretches of water. She's even given it a tiny sitting area all its own with a pretty round table piled with curvaceous Moorish boxes of wood and metal. There's a kilim under the table to define the special sitting area, and old kilims have been made into cushion covers – that's the Moroccan influence. The floors in this room are stained white beech, adding even more light to the combined reflections of sun and water.

The care that has been taken over the detailing of the floors in each room gives the house its unique flavour. In the entrance hall, where visitors are immediately introduced to Fern Mallis's love of collecting, the floor is a deep reddish black. There is a row of tiny chairs, made both for children and as apprentice pieces, and a whole series of fern specimens, all limey-green fronds and deep-cut silhouettes. The dark, nearly black planking runs through into the open-plan living area, where floor rugs take up the monochrome scheme. This is further emphasized by a series of black-and-white

striped bowls, which she also collects. All the snatches of colour come from incidentals, making it possible to change the feeling of a room entirely between summer and winter. Towards the end of summer there are vases of brilliant yellow sunflowers, posies of daisies and large bowls filled with nothing but foliage. Vegetables are equally effective – with, for example, yellow tomatoes arranged in the black-and-white bowls, or fresh green and yellow sweetcorn in a natural basket. A score of lime-green apples and pears sit in an antique wooden bowl.

Cushions and throws are another device to add splashes of colour. Scarlet oriental-style throws are casually draped over the colonial bed, and striped fabrics act as cushions on the high chairs around the kitchen counter. In summer, even the outside wooden jetty gets a bright mix of coloured fabrics, which look artlessly

beautiful when seen from above, from the upper rooms. An American flag drapes an outdoor dining table, with shockingly clashing pink watermelon slices above its scarlet stripes.

Fern Mallis says her intention is to emphasize the qualities of the house while making the décor ideal for entertaining and relaxing. When you hear her talk about what she is trying to achieve – what she does achieve – it creates a potent fantasy, redolent of the atmosphere that we are all trying to create in our homes, whether for the weekend or every day. 'I stained the floors dark and slip-covered much of the furniture in white. I bought a lot of the pieces in the country at various places, looking out for different woods which were both warm and appropriate. The house is accessorized with my enormous miniature chair collection, kilim pillows, ikat pillows, Picasso print pillows, cashmere and other throws. All of it is about

OPPOSITE PAGE Waterside locations are almost always green because they rarely suffer from drought. Fern Mallis has managed to evoke the colours of the land outside the house in her collection of ferny botanical specimens – just one of her passions. Another passion is tiny children's and apprentice chairs.

ABOVE The main bedroom in the cottage has splendid views over the lake, whose fleeting colours are enhanced by the monochrome shades of the room, with its statuesque colonial half-tester bed and stained beech floor. The set of library steps provides a means of climbing up onto the bed should jumping fail.

THIS PAGE **The skills involved in decorating these luscious homes include knowing when to use colour and when to avoid it. Fern Mallis loves the natural colours of flowers, fruit and vegetables. Here she has arranged watermelon slices on a black-and-white dish set on a table covered with the bright primary colours of the American flag. This provides the only bright spot in a garden vista (below), where a leaning branch frames a glimpse of the table among the hydrangeas with the lake shimmering beyond.**

OPPOSITE PAGE **The colours of the log pile and potting shed look supremely natural, as does an old woven-wood chair – but such simplicity is achieved only with guile.**

being comfortable, laying back, reading, watching endless movies on TV or, in summer, sitting outside and enjoying the lake and the sun. All the paintings in the house are by my dad, my sisters or my nieces.'

The garden is as important in this scheme as the house. It, too, is carefully controlled to evoke long-gone summers, relaxation, parties and fun. It leads down to the lake and its old wooden jetty with a moored canoe, and is so heavily wooded that, from the water, the house seems to peep out through the canopy of leaves.

The house's coy façade, shingled and painted white, is infinitely welcoming, with generous verandahs, windows scattered throughout and a series of paths and steps leading up from the water's edge. There are areas of the garden where sawn logs are stored for winter fires and where old-fashioned terracotta pots sit on shelves waiting to be potted up with summer-blooming scented flowers. Everywhere there are American classic chairs made of curved branches and bleached by the sun, or of painted planks reclined for maximum comfort. Lanterns are hung on posts to light at night, while shaded candles are ready for the outdoor dining table.

There is nothing here that will not give pleasure. Anything ugly is banned, as is anything work-related. This house by the freshwater lake is all about hedonism after travail. And it works. 'I get more pleasure out of two days here on a weekend than I ever knew possible,' says Fern Mallis. 'Just watching the water and the way the sun or moon reflect on the surface, the wind or the ice in winter. I can stare at it for hours and never be bored. I feel as if my batteries are recharged just by being here – and my batteries do get depleted after a typical work week. I enjoy being here all year round to watch and feel the seasons change, to feel the whole, to sleep late and do nothing. To be here and see many friends. Or to be here and see no one.'

serenity in the forest

In a remote part of Maine teeming with
moose and bear, birds and fish, a
house built of spruce logs from
the nearby forest stands serenely
on the shores of a long lake.

It is hard for Europeans to comprehend that there are still virtually
unexplored areas of wilderness in the USA. There are huge lakes,
acres of dense forest and towering mountains that were once the
hunting grounds of the American Indians and, later, the solitary
preserves of trappers, pioneer farmers and hunters. Paul and Melba
Chodosh discovered their own wilderness as long ago as 1946. It is
a full day's drive from their present apartment in Lower Manhattan,
but that does not deter them. Indeed, based in New York all winter,
they pine for its solitude and long for the spring to bring them back.

Their holding is in Maine on the shores of a long, active lake.
The area teems with moose and bear, birds and fish. 'It's been a long
love affair,' says Mel. They first found the area in 1946, and went
back regularly until, in 1960, they bought their first house, or 'camp'
as they call it. Three years after that they bought a second camp, and
this has been their family home ever since. The house was built

in the early 20th century entirely by hand from spruce logs, which were also peeled by hand and put into place with a pulley, horses and manpower. 'The builder would have first cleared the land of spruces, which were then probably used to build the house. Then he would have lived alone there. It was just a one-room log cabin with a well and a sink. He was a French Canadian and clearly a good designer because the plan was great.

'He later built two or three other houses for people who lived here during the hunting and fishing season. It must have been a very hard life because it gets very, very cold in winter: –30˚F (–34˚C). The lake freezes solid, and there's a hotel nearby that still cuts ice from the lake to cool the icehouse where they store food. There was only liquor and wood stoves to keep them warm, and we know the French Canadian died poor and a drunk. He never enjoyed the benefits of his work and talent.'

OPPOSITE PAGE, ABOVE
The family have known the waters of this huge and unpopulated lake in Maine since 1946. They bought their second 'camp' there in 1963.

OPPOSITE PAGE, INSET
The main house of the camp dates from about 1900, and has recently had a formal staircase to the door and verandah added. It is one of six buildings that made up the original property.

ABOVE LEFT **Log-cabin construction has been used for the inner walls of the wide, comfortable verandah of the old house. It looks out over the lake and is a perfect setting for family parties.**

ABOVE RIGHT **The sauna, which also has a fine view of the lake, is built of rough logs like the house. A 'no hunting' sign is not simply a joke: hunting is strictly controlled in the area.**

THIS PAGE **The family still catch and grill the landlocked salmon and rainbow trout that live in the lake, where stocks are now rising. In nooks and crannies all over the property are little reminders of ships and water.**

OPPOSITE PAGE **Mel and Paul are keen to preserve the rustic character of their wilderness home: the old chairs on the verandah are well worn and comfortable with bleached cotton cushions, while tables, chairs and table lamps seem to be constructed from local driftwood and branches with their bark left on.**

This primitive house in a wilderness has taken over the lives of Paul and Mel because it has become an integral part of the family. Their honeymoon was spent in the area rather than in this particular house, but since then the simple building has seen the arrival of their five children, their children's spouses and, latterly, their 11 grandchildren and two step-grandchildren. 'It's a focal point for family gatherings, children, husbands, wives and their children. It's a very major part of our lives. It's what we're really all about.'

Since Paul retired as an ear, nose and throat surgeon in New York 12 years ago, they have spent more time here than ever. 'We are here from May to November.' More recently still, the couple hired the architect Stephen Blatt to enlarge their holding and, to Mel's relief, increase the kitchen size.

Blatt explains what was behind the changes: 'After 30 years of benign, respectful nurturing of the six original buildings, the family, having previously commissioned us for work elsewhere, initially sought help to renovate the kitchen. Mel, a gourmet cook, wanted a facility better equipped than the original "summer" kitchen, better integrated with the house, with views to the lake and a place to eat and schmooze in rare moments with no guests or family in tow.

'This "small project" became an adventure in architectural "neo-archaeology" as we proceeded together looking at the entire house, then the entire compound.'

So the whole kitchen was moved and made bigger, while the old kitchen became a studio where Mel works as a potter. 'The new, enlarged, reorientated kitchen is more accessible from the driveway, to the dining room and other support spaces,' says Blatt. 'This new kitchen generated an entirely new circulation scheme through the house, including a new front door, mudroom, laundry room and office. A guest room was tucked above along a support spine, lined floor to ceiling with bookshelves.'

Mel simply finds that there is now lots more space. Where once her children would perch on the worktops – 'there was never any place for cooking, it was impossible to push them aside, and you could never eat there, only in the dining room' – there is now ample work space. 'I had great pleasure in planning the kitchen. It's very, very long, a really difficult space, but my plan works.'

Blatt then decided to give the old house a courtyard. 'The relocated kitchen-now-studio received a new porch, facing the

'We tried to make the additions fit in with the original and to look as though they'd always been there. It's a wonderful place for entertaining. The main porch will fit a hundred people standing.'

new kitchen's porch and an existing porch on the guest bunkhouse. All these create a social courtyard of singular charm.'

This is just as well, because the couple seem to spend a great deal of time entertaining at this lovely old house. 'All the children and grandchildren come when they can, and we can put them up quite easily. If there are too many of them to fit into the house, then they put up tents in the woods and on the lakeside. We've never run out of space.

'There's an outhouse in the field and another small house on the property, which means we can sleep quite a few families. We can put up four families in the house quite comfortably and even fit in five.' As a result, all major family reunions take place beside the lake, which she describes as 'tranquil and beautiful'.

The whole area is under a preservation order that stipulates that the lake should be kept as wild as it was when the Norridgewick, part of the Abenaki people, hunted around its shores. 'Our lake is very large, and when we first moved here its shores were unpopulated. We first rented a cottage in an American Plan Camp, where you stay in log cabins with a fireplace but no kitchen and are given three meals a day. The fishing was good and, though we didn't fish at first, we learned to. The place was so peaceful and back-to-nature – it made an absolute change from our daily

ABOVE **It can get extremely cold out on the lakeside in the depths of winter, and a log fire (supplemented by efficient heating) draws the family to the old hearth. The stairs beside it lead up to the bedrooms, while decoy ducks, old guns and rubble-stone walls combine to recreate the atmosphere of traditional log-cabin life.**

OPPOSITE PAGE **Wood is the main fuel out in these forests, and along with open fires the house has wood-burning stoves, like this one in the sauna overlooking the lake. Mel is a potter, and her bowls, put on tables with tiles also made by her, are filled with colourful fruit. A cut-tin lantern casts shadows on the wall at night.**

lives. There was the opportunity to garden. Then we were able to teach the children things that were impossible in the city – they became boatsmen, they learned to swim and practise the simple life. They could see the stars without bright city lights.'

Although there has been some development around the lake, the area is still remote and wild and, thanks to the protection laws, will remain so for ever.

We have moose, bear, deer, bald eagles and peregrine falcons. The moose are a problem, and under state law people can hunt them once a year by lottery. It's not difficult to kill them because they stand as still as cows. You can eat moose and some people stuff their heads – which I think is quite horrible.

Moose are controlled because they cause so many road accidents. 'Even if you drive at 25 miles an hour, if you hit one you'll probably kill it, and, even if you get out in one piece, the collision will destroy your car. Yet it's wonderful living in this wild country. The moose are huge, with enormous racks of antlers. They are beautiful in the summer, but in spring they look just awful because they moult.'

'Black bear were seen often years ago because there were open areas for garbage dumps. When those went, they went. Now the bear are coming back again – no one can understand why. Although they've always been hunted here, they are not really

THE HOUSE WAS BUILT IN THE EARLY 20TH CENTURY ENTIRELY BY HAND FROM SPRUCE LOGS, WHICH WERE ALSO PEELED BY HAND AND PUT INTO PLACE WITH A PULLEY, HORSES AND MANPOWER.

dangerous unless you come between a cub and its mother or remove food that they are planning to eat. Then they can even come into your house if they get hungry.'

So the wilderness out in Maine is quite real, and beyond the lake the high Appalachians create a rugged backdrop. The lake itself provides fish for their meals. 'We've had good fishing again – the fish did decline a while ago, but we've asked scientists how to make it better and the fish have come back. We have landlocked salmon and rainbow trout, which we catch and grill for ourselves – we're not allowed to sell them.'

In tune with this simple life, Paul and Mel elected to keep their home as simple as their surroundings. Stephen Blatt comments, 'Our overriding challenge was to make the additions work and fit. Comfort remains the order of the day here; elegance and charm

have fortuitously joined in. Various subtle touches were applied, including a bay window off the dining room, which opens the room both functionally and perceptually. New French doors leading from the dining room to the screen porch encourage alfresco dining.'

Mel adds, 'We tried to make the additions fit in with the original and to look as though they'd always been there. It's a wonderful place for entertaining. The main porch will fit a hundred people standing. We have buffet meals there and, though there is electricity, we use candles at night.'

The love affair is by no means over. 'There are so few people here and we can't even see our neighbour's house. It's truly idyllic, a make-believe place. The world isn't this way any more. We feel extremely grateful and privileged to be here and we thank whoever made it happen every day.'

summer camp revisited

Amid woods smelling of pine needles, where moose or bear might emerge at any moment from behind the next tree trunk, red flannel hash and burgers were seared over smoking hickory wood.

In 20th-century Britain, some people got rid of their children for long periods – if they could afford it – by sending them to boarding school for three quarters of the year. In North America, where, as in much of Europe, such a tradition did not exist, adults were given a tiny bit of freedom when they sent their children to summer camps.

The idea was that, fresh from the city and the crowded prison of school, where life involved little that was more arduous than a bus ride or a ball game, the children would be introduced to nature, the real thing, without sanitizing comforts. Summer camps were established all over the continent with a single aim: that they should be in the real country with real flora and fauna for the youngsters to contend with. Children were treated like boy scouts and girl guides, taught how to tie knots, cook a – probably charred – meal over a camp fire, and wash in cold water poured from an old bucket.

Curiously, this treatment evokes in Americans the same longing that Englishmen feel for the steak-and-kidney pudding and 'dead man's leg', the jam-and-suet dish they were given as ten-year-olds in prep schools. It may have seemed quite horrible at the time but, with hindsight, summer camp recalls for American children a time when the woods smelled of pine needles, when moose and bear just might be around the next tree trunk, and when meals of red flannel hash and burgers, cooked over smoking hickory wood, were the most delicious foods in the world.

How else can one explain the mass exodus of sophisticated New Yorkers and Manhattanites to the true wilderness? Why else would these smart folk, who daily wear shined black brogues or kitten-heeled patent leathers, be willing to trade in the comfort of central heating, a myriad smart restaurants, cinema and theatre, in return for log cabins and rustic furniture that can eat opaque tights as easily as a shark gnaws a leg?

The pioneering bit – playing for a while at being a fur trapper for the Hudson's Bay Company, or an Indian scout, or a farmer ready to clear and burn his own patch for growing corn – digs deep into the

OPPOSITE PAGE **One pleasure of living by a lake is the choice of hidden corners that can be adapted for alfresco meals. A cheerful blue-and-white gingham cloth on a table flanked by Adirondack chairs is neatly outside the kitchen door. It's set for a casual lunch with white china and cut white flowers in a pretty vase.**

THIS PAGE **Rough twigs from the surrounding forests along with logs and bleached decking create a gazebo attached to the house and at the far end of the verandah. This overlooks the waters of the lake.**

American psyche. While the French or Italians are still resistant to the idea of a country retreat, despite the sharp edge of rude Parisians and the humidity and mosquitoes of Florence, Americans have more northerly blood in them. They, like the Swedes, take to the water each spring and summer, after the ice has melted and before the gnats start to bite; they dream in winter of the first shoots of spring and the unfolding violets, as we do in Britain; they are keen to exercise their dogs and hunt game as they do in Germany.

Added to this is the fact that the USA has some of the last true wildernesses in the Western world. Alexandra Champalimaud, an interior designer, and her businessman husband Bruce can depart from the centre of New York and, within an hour of leaving the boundaries of suburbia, find themselves in such an untouched slice of nature. In a couple of hours they can cross the divide between one of the most urban landscapes on earth, New York City, where the sun is lost between canyons of buildings, and rural Connecticut, where the silence is overwhelming and nature is totally in control. There are few other Western countries where such a contrast can be found in such a short space of time.

ABOVE **The kitchen ceiling is hung with dozens of striped paper lanterns that tend to sway in the wind.**

OPPOSITE PAGE **Alexandra Champalimaud was far too clever to cover over the graffiti created by earlier visitors to the camp, who painted and scrawled their names all over the kitchen walls and doors. They add greatly to the atmosphere.**

BELOW LEFT **The main bedroom has been arranged and decorated with great simplicity, while its generous windows allow the light to flood in and provide wide views over the water.**

BELOW **Curved branches, found in the nearby woods, give the impression of holding up the rough stone fireplace – although of course in reality they don't.**

In Britain there is no wilderness to speak of – and two hours' driving from central London will take you no farther than the well-populated counties of Suffolk or Sussex. Drive a couple of hours from Paris or Rome and you will still be among agricultural fields, charming villages and advertisement hoardings. You will be fortunate if you see a wild bird or any animal more unusual than a fallow deer or a fox. But travel the same distance from a big city in the USA and you are deep in forests that are as nearly untouched as when the American Indian tribes hunted bear and made their canoes from the bark of the forest birch trees.

After the Indians, emigrants from Europe began to carve out their territories in these forests. They would built log cabins using the straight trunks of the trees they had cleared to hack out the first vegetable beds; they might introduce a few cows, pigs or hens to provide food – and, of course, they would fish in the deep lakes for the abundant freshwater varieties of shellfish and trout.

THIS PAGE AND OPPOSITE
The living-room floor, walls and ceiling are made of natural wood. and some of the furniture has survived from the time when the place was a camp. One end of the living room leads to the main bedroom, while the other opens into a hallway whose doors open onto a verandah.

OPPOSITE, SMALL PICTURES
American pioneers copied the northern European habit of painting furniture in soft colours. Here a bluey-green side table is set against the untouched wood of the living-room walls, against which boating pictures are propped. Other tablescapes include an old fan, a lamp perched on a pile of of books, and local finds such as pheasant feathers, a stag's antler and an old Coca-Cola bottle.

Luckily, nowadays it's possible to have the enjoyment of the wilderness – the brilliant stars undimmed by city lights, the silence of the forests broken by the eerie cries of nature's hunters and hunted, the soft lapping of the water – with the added bonus of central heating, air conditioning in summer, effective screens against mosquitoes, and a four-wheel-drive car to make short work of the trip from Manhattan to Connecticut.

Camp Kent, 30 years ago, was a place for children set beside the shores of a typically forested lake in the north of the country. In its heyday it had consisted of a large group of clapboard buildings clustered around the shores; these were intended as dormitories and recreational buildings for the children who arrived every summer. But such camps were going out of favour with the American public who, instead, were becoming avid for a piece of wild nature all their own. Planning laws and controls over building, altering the wilderness or creating the infrastructure people need today were becoming increasingly strict, to the extent that it was quite often impossible to develop new collections of buildings in particularly lovely areas. One solution was to find run-down houses, put up in a less strict era, and transform them into weekend homes for today.

Alexandra Champalimaud's husband found Camp Kent at a time when it was beginning to decline. 'The camp had been going for 30 years with about 50 red clapboard buildings with white trim dotted above a beach and dock. The owner/manager of the camp had aged sufficiently to want to slow down his summer schedule,' she explains now.

'While local zoning laws theoretically permitted several hundred condominiums to be constructed on the property, the owner was only prepared to sell to someone who would change the property minimally. My future husband and a couple of friends could not resist this little corner of Connecticut, lost down a dirt road, but less than two hours from Manhattan.'

The whole group of buildings was in a pretty bad state, having had three decades of fierce storms and icy winters to weather, but the position was superb. 'The crumbling camp buildings were removed, except for the five that had life in them. A compound was created around a big barn overhanging the lake, which had long served as the Camp Kent theatre. This theatre is now the soul of our retreat.'

The clapboarded main house has no fewer than eight bedrooms. There are also a guesthouse with a further two bedrooms and the Adirondack-style cabin which can fit in another seven guests. The whole is set in 6 hectares (15 acres) of wilderness. It is therefore not unknown for 24 colleagues, friends and family to meet here for a weekend away from it all.

Luckily, Alexandra loves entertaining — when she's not revamping the Algonquin hotel, decorating a couple of houses in Aspen or building another home in New Mexico. 'I can organize food for 20 in two minutes,' she says. 'I grew up in a house that was constantly full, so I got used to it.'

Creating the whole holiday home, however, was not so instant. 'Before the camp became a home, we spent hours prospecting and redesigning — trying to make sense of the assemblage of rustic camp bunks, the music room, the old infirmary and the nearly collapsed theatre.

'While I tried to add my energy and "edge" to my new friends' vision and enthusiasm, our children forged their friendships through theatricals and

OPPOSITE PAGE **There are lots of places to relax by the lake – both indoors and out. A hammock is casually slung between trees, while a guest bedroom's walls reach only to the rafters, leaving empty space above for ventilation and inter-room conversations.**

OPPOSITE PAGE AND BELOW **One feature of the house is the repeated use of rough but charmingly curved**

branches retrieved from the nearby woodland. In these rooms they prop up a shelf for books sited above a bed and decorate a tiny angle between the wooden walls of a bath and a shower.

LEFT **Imaginative use of decking is in evidence throughout the property. Here it is used to create a boat jetty that supports wooden lounging chairs.**

productions of their own in the Camp Kent theatre which was, at that time, complete with moth-eaten costumes and sweeping faded red curtains.'

Alexandra Champalimaud has been extremely careful not to lose any of the charm of this ancient group of buildings hidden down a track. 'The style, if you can call it that, is simplified Adirondack, with a branch – bark and all – holding the shower curtain, for example. I chose to change the red and white vernacular to dark red with brown/black trim because we learned that the natural and dark colours "disappeared" into the woods around – even in the leafless Connecticut winter.'

Most of the rooms are timber clad with the planks arrayed horizontally, as in all the best log cabins. Indeed, the rooms are cubes of timber with planked and beamed ceilings, and floors of yet more planks. None is painted. The furniture also appears basic. The chairs look as though they were made by a pioneer working with bare branches, while pictures are propped on shelves more often than hung. Colours everywhere are soft and subtle – whites, creams, off-whites, bleached woods, a touch of Swedish green on a painted table. Equally, the family impedimenta are used for decoration. There are feathers and old bottles, electric table fans and a room dominated by old khaki waders. And the lake is brought into the whole scheme by a long, planked jetty where the kayak is moored and, in summer, lounging cabin chairs are arrayed to take advantage of the view.

One of the main features, says Alexandra Champalimaud, is the walls, where long-departed holiday children once daubed their names along with whorls and stars. 'If Camp Kent has a single memorable detail,' she says, 'it's the names of generations of campers scrawled in paint that remains in the kitchen – plus the names of our family and friends who have worked on weekends to help us bring the theatre back to life. As our families fell in

love with each other, this little lake filled with drinking-quality water became more than a swimming/fishing dock to us.' It became an integral part of their lives, a place which held the soul of their family. 'With the abundant wildlife and nearly pure wilderness just an hour beyond the boundaries of suburbia, Camp Kent became as equally magical as any habitable place for us . . . my sons, my daughters and all our friends.'

Their intense involvement in its magic and its purity has made the family determined to preserve this remote corner of Connecticut. 'It retains that children's summer-camp feeling that brings a smile to every face. The theatre is the ultimate party barn in the summer and a broom-hockey or ping-pong room on those frigid winter days.

'Camp Kent remains a camp for all ages of the family and our friends which is shared with abundant wild life – beaver, otters, wild turkey, deer, eagles, hawks, ruffled grouse and the occasional black bear or coyote – along with all the little creatures of the New England woods. The lake is full of bass and pike, along with freshwater prawns and mussels. There is a great trout stream only ten minutes away.'

One of their neighbours is a professional hydrologist who has made it his business to ensure that the purity of the water – which can be drunk directly from the lake – is never lost. 'He patrols daily in his wet suit. When I pass him in my kayak he can provide a report on his latest measurement of water purity. We allow no motors on the lake, and take every available precaution that his measurements never signal damage from the presence of the community. The local ice fishermen help preserve the area too, and their little shacks represent an enjoyable alternative to a local pub at the end of a winter walk.'

At the back of the lake are the forests. 'The woodlands, wetlands and meadows provide us with all the pleasures of the four full seasons in the New England woods. While the fall colours are world famous, and early spring is a study in delicacy, most spectacular is the June explosion of pink mountain laurel on the ledges of the hillsides that run down to the lake – except perhaps when the icy winter arrives quickly on a windless day, freezing the lake into a clear sheet of glass through which you can see to the bottom of the lake. Last year we enjoyed a spectacular, sunny afternoon skating across the top of this crystal aquarium.'

THIS PAGE AND OPPOSITE
People who make their homes beside water must be well prepared to deal with the elements. This means lots of special equipment, from sunproof hats – to cut the double glare of the sunshine reflecting on the lake's surface – to heavy-duty waders for people who fish. A whole array of waders and skating boots, rubber boots and anti-mosquito hats are lined up in the house's hallway, which has been given over to a decorative scheme of hanging outfits and a suitably cheery welcome board.

After the fire, Lynn was
allowed to rebuild on the
same 'footprint' and decided
that everything should look
as if it had been there for
ever. Wooden shingles cover
the outside verandah walls,
with chairs and other
woodwork painted Shaker
blue, while Adirondack chairs
stand on plain bleached-
wood floors. The dog, like
everyone who comes here,
loves the lure of the lakeside.

fire and ice in Maine

It would be hard to guess that this house replaces an earlier version that literally blew up after a lightning strike within a few months of the new owner moving in.

Lynn, a photographer, knows all about the problems of owning a house on a remote lake shore. The first accident that happened to her old cottage in Maine was, it is true, only tenuously connected with water, in that storms and gales often seem to be worse near water. One June day in 1992 – when, luckily, she was away – the trees around her house were struck by lightning.

Lynn had bought the place the previous August. She had spent three weekends there that first summer and another two or three the following spring.

'I was planning to be there in the summer and feel my way through what to do with the cottage – whether to winterize it. I wasn't there that June day but I'm told that the trees around were struck and the house literally blew up. It was the force of the

electricity – or whatever it was in the lightning – that went through the tree roots and under the house, which was on stilts against flooding. The whole thing just ignited. It was totally demolished.'

Eight years later, and after a prolonged pause for thought, she admits that, now, she's glad it happened. 'The fact that it burned down changed a lot for me. Without that, I might not have moved here. It was actually worse, in a way, to lose the trees.'

The fire gave Lynn the chance to start again and rebuild on the same site, a mere 2 metres (6 ft) from the water's edge. If it had not occurred she would have been allowed neither to extend the tiny cottage nor to pull it down and rebuild. But the state authorities agreed that she could create another house, provided that it was on exactly the same 'footprint' as the old house's frontage. At the

Who could resist placing a
carved wooden swan by the
living-room windows which
overlook the waters of the
lake? Here, as in the rest of
the house, colours are
subordinated to the views:
the chairs are upholstered in
neutrals; natural wickerwork
baskets for storage are
ranged above white wood-
planked cupboards in the
bathroom, while translucent
white curtains shade its
windows. Everywhere there
are comfy old chairs
cushioned in well-washed
fabrics, well-used shoes and
moccasins for walking, and
lake-washed pebbles.

back she was given a bit more leeway, and she was allowed to build upwards. Her chosen architect was Stephen Blatt, and her instructions were quite clear: she wanted the new house 'to look as though it had always been there'. The result was so successful that the cottage won Blatt an Honor Award from the Maine Chapter of the American Institute of Architects in 1995 and, in 2000, another from the New England Design Awards.

'We were commissioned to replace the cottage, not with a replica but with a year-round home providing the equivalent amount of peace, quiet and memories,' says Stephen Blatt. 'Land-use regulation allowed rebuilding on the old footprint with conditions: no more than 25% expansion, 30% volume expansion.

'The original one-storey structure contained minimal volume under a simple roof. In order to abide by the footprint limitation, bedrooms are on an upper level. Under the gables, porches surround the house; their depth, especially at the corners, is enunciated by the shallow pitch of the perimeter roofs. Windows are small and simple and the detailing is straightforward and rugged.

'One approaches the house from deep woods, passing a small guesthouse guarding the site. One is beckoned by broad sitting steps leading up to a sheltered porch and a screened dining porch. Upstairs a guest room faces north, while the owner's bedroom suite has water views in three directions, with morning light to the bathtub, southerly views down the lake and sunset in a small reading nook.' Wonderful.

The first cottage was meant to be 'a weekend getaway', says Lynn. 'It could not be lived in without modifications. It was a maximum of 1000 square feet.' The new 'cottage' has now become her main home, with a second home in California, where her mother and sister live. And, yes, commuting between the wilderness and San Francisco does amount to culture shock.

'I've lived here by the lake since 1995 and it's fabulous.' One reason is the constant changes wrought by the water. 'The lake freezes in winter and the ice is usually covered in snow – so we do lots of skiing and other activities on the water. My dog, a black labrador called BJ, just loves to run around on the ice. Then ice fishermen come and put up shacks all around us. It's not very picturesque but we have a lot of laughs watching what they get up to – drinking beer and slapping each other on the back.' There are bass, perch, landlocked salmon and trout in the lake (though she buys her fish from a store rather than catch it herself) and colourful water birds. 'The loons are the principal birds here.

They're large and not too good on land, so they mostly need to paddle. They nest by the shore, but we do our best to leave them alone. We try to protect them from the motorboats that threaten their environment. They are magnificent to look at – black with white accent feathers.'

Other wildfowl make the lake a migratory stop. Bufflehead ducks and hooded mergansers come in their hundreds and may stay for only a day. 'The state bird is the chickadee – we have them, as well as bluebirds and redwing blackbirds. We have native blueberry and huckleberry bushes, and the birds eat their berries. There are deer in the area, and moose have been sighted here – I've seen footprints in the front yard. An otter lives on the property. There are wild turkeys, and beavers came two years ago.'

The beavers proceeded to cut down one of the poplar trees – apparently their favourite – but so far the wonderful pines, hemlocks and cedar evergreens, along with the oaks, maples, beeches and birches that cluster on the point, have survived intact.

The weather is the opposite of what Lynn experiences in California. 'It can be very windy and stormy but also quite lovely, magnificent. One phenomenon that happens in April is that the ice breaks up in the lake and flows with the current to one end. A couple of years ago the wind changed as this was happening and started pushing the ice to the north, up to my house. The ice piled up all around the shore and I was afraid it was going to come up onto the porch. It was extraordinary – in little pieces like ice cubes, piling up towards me and tinkling as they rolled over . . . bizarre and scary.'

When the ice is intact, however, and as long as the snow hasn't fallen, she can skate along the lake as far as the little local town, which is reached by sailing boat in summer. 'My boat is very easy to sail because it is so small. It takes an absolute maximum of three. I've also taken a fishing boat with a motor to the town

and paddled a canoe there. There's a little place where we can eat, so we go there in summer.'

In summer, too, Lynn and her friends eat out on an open porch (carefully screened with mesh against mosquitoes). 'The house's design makes it very easy to have meals there because it's next to the dining area and just as close to the kitchen.'

Lynn also works from the house – she's a photographer creating fine-art prints. 'I sell prints for people's offices and living rooms.' And she takes pictures of her particular stretch of lake, which is 18 km (11 miles) long in total, in all its moods.

Since the terrible day of the lightning strike the trees and underbrush have grown back, and the house is settling down to look even more mature and established. Perhaps it was a lucky strike after all.

'The lake freezes in winter and the ice is usually covered in snow – so we do a lot of skiing and other activities on the water. My black labrador just loves to run around on the ice. Then ice fishermen come and put up shacks all around us.'

OPPOSITE PAGE **Lynn's black labrador is called BJ and his favourite days are spent on the shores of the huge lake, where he can gambol and swim. He needs to be de-mudded, however, before coming into the cosy rooms. Wooden floors, though, are less inimical to muddy footprints.**

THIS PAGE **The bed in Lynn's room (above right) is covered in a favourite blanket from her mother and a newer one from Ralph Lauren, while the tiny guest room has a fine log-cabin quilt on the bed (right).**

riverside living

Riverside living offers much more variety than you might expect. From thundering torrent to placid flow, from mountain stream to lazy estuary, all riverside locations have one thing in common: a sense of the water's journey from its source to the sea.

The river dwellers in this section may be within minutes of the centre of Paris, perched above a sleepy Devon inlet on England's south coast, ranging the rivers of Europe by boat – or looking down on one of the most exciting views in the world. That's riverside living for you.

Roderick James has fishing and water in his genes, and can mess about in boats all day, every day from a house on a creek in Devon. His house, Seagull House, is also an expression of his architectural passion for working in oak, as did the medieval builders of England's early houses. Clients, queueing up for his designs, must visit him here to see its potential.

The Dorroughs – he an architect, she an artist – live and work in a house he designed on a historic Australian island, Dangar Island, which is within commuting distance of Sydney. The living space is so flexible that there are decks, verandahs and porches on all sides to catch the views and the light every minute of the day and night. Meanwhile, Peter and Tonia live in

an exciting modern space high above Sydney Harbour, with one of the most famous views in the world wrapped all around them. Since discovering the house on the waterside virtually by accident, they find that waterside living has completely changed their lives.

An old island shack, its walls painted with realistic fish by previous occupants who were fishermen, has been turned by the Australian architect Les Reedman into a cleverly interchangeable space for dreaming, swimming and fishing – and, of course, eating and sleeping. There's even a bathroom with views of the Hawkesbury river.

Rupert Morgan threw up the day job (and the expensive London property prices) to become a novelist, writing from his old Dutch boat, a 50-tonne steel Tjaalk, in which he has crossed the seas and journeyed all over France. Now, in deference to his young children, it's moored on the Seine waiting for them to grow up and enjoy travelling with the house alongside.

Friends thought a Parisian fashion desiger had gone mad when she left dry land to live on a houseboat on the Seine minutes from the centre of the capital. Now, when they see the charming French rooms and decking garden, the cruising ducks and swans, they're not so sure they were right.

a work of art in wood

Overlooking a tidal creek in south-west England, amid lusciously green valleys, is a timber-framed house that was rebuilt using traditional crafts dating back 700 years.

Everyone in the know about house-buying says that the secret is location, location, location – for the panoramic view, the silence of the countryside or the soft murmur of the sea is the one part of a house that cannot be changed. And, although it might at first seem desirable to look for the most historical and architecturally magnificent house you can find, it is worth keeping an open mind, especially since there is so much exciting new architecture around.

The problems of old buildings are not just those of conservation and repair. In many countries of Europe, official regulations prevent new owners from changing important buildings to suit modern needs. Windows, for example, cannot be enlarged; doors cannot be glazed; rooflines must remain as they have always been; and staircases cannot be replaced. So clever buyers often look for run-down, even ugly houses, generally dating from the period between the 1930s

THIS PAGE AND OPPOSITE Seagull House was once an undistinguished block of a house – until Roderick James got to work on its shell. The family have now been living, working – and playing – at the edge of the water for more than 12 years. Roderick effectively 'bungalow-ate' the old house, having bought it for its location rather than for any aesthetic attributes. Verandahs were built all around the original building to create a series of sheltered, semi-outdoor rooms at ground level, while on the upper level each bedroom gained an outdoor platform to allow occupants to take full advantage of the beautiful views.

and the 1970s, which had been built in wonderful situations that were then less valued. They may have been badly built from cheap materials, because few people who could afford more comfortable homes thought it desirable to shiver in the howling gales of cliff and creek.

Modern transport has put the most isolated house within reach of big cities, while modern technology – in glass, for example – means that great views over rivers and creeks are easily inserted in place of older, smaller windows. Central heating takes care of cold; insulation stops the draughts that once whistled under every window and door. The planners may even beg you to pull down the excrescences and start again, removing asbestos, ugly roofing and jerry-building.

This was exactly what Roderick James did with his house – with one crucial difference. Instead of using ultra-modern techniques with concrete and

glass, he went back 700 years to find a technology that is just as elegant and adaptable as the highest tech building of the 21st century. He went for medieval timber framing.

Seagull House was once a plain house with little to distinguish it – but that was before 1988, when Roderick and his wife Gillie moved in with their three sons, Daniel, Ben and Woody. They had come from Gloucestershire to the far West Country – a long way, in English terms – for a single, simple reason (apart from the adventure of creating a new home), and that was the house's position. It stands high above a tidal creek in Devon amid lusciously green wooded valleys that climb steeply up from the water.

James is an architect who, as Roderick James Architects, has been in practice since 1974 working with oak barns (having converted his first in Wales in 1973, where he was director of the Centre for

ABOVE LEFT **One of the spare bedrooms has this nautically themed bathroom en suite. The walls are made of very rough sawn boards, with marine caulk used in between. It is like being in an old wooden ship.**

ABOVE **Everywhere in Seagull House, seagoing ephemera and objects are positioned to reflect the waterside location. This cheerful little lighthouse model is, in fact, a tiny tit-nesting box with a perch.**

Alternative Technology). He is also in partnership with a friend, Charles Brentnall, in the firm Carpenter Oak and Woodland, which creates new timber-framed buildings using traditional crafts with a contemporary spin. James is the designer and Brentnall is the expert in timber and its construction – though, after so many years, their combined expertise is almost certainly as great as that of the medieval builders who created whole towns from oak trees.

It all came about because Roderick James was concerned about the spate of barn conversions in which great and ancient spaces throughout the country were clumsily carved up into family homes. Careless conversion, he felt, resulted in 'the loss of drama and space'.

Yet he understood the modern demand for dramatic open-plan homes in the countryside, and wanted to offer the same theatricality in houses

ABOVE LEFT **The muted colours and designs that characterize the interior of the house itself are offset by bright fabrics, casually slung.**

ABOVE RIGHT **A painter and quiltmaker, Gillie James has a studio in the house. The walls are adorned with examples of her work.**

BELOW **The family may have up to ten boats on the creek at any one time, for sailing or enjoying a relaxing session on the water. Directly below the house, at water level, are a boathouse and a workshop for boat repairs. Seafaring is in the family's blood. James's ancestors captained barques and brigantines.**

constructed from scratch for a modern way of life. The firm now has four separate yards, from Devon to Scotland, and employs no fewer than 60 carpenters.

Seagull House, designed and built by Roderick James with both his hats on, is rather more traditional than his current work. It serves as not only a family home but also a place to talk to clients and demonstrate what can be done with wood and building techniques that have been practised in England and Wales for more than seven centuries. Since he is currently working on no fewer than 45 projects, both for complete buildings and for extensions, he likes his clients to make the commitment of journeying to Devon to show him that they are serious. They are in

for a treat. Seagull House is very different from the 1950s block that the James family took on. The house now consists of the original building 'bungalow-eaten' with wooden cladding, clinker-built for a fine nautical effect and enlivened by a ground-level verandah and a first-floor balcony. Then there is a new, full-scale timber-framed 'barn' using trusses, beams and joints developed in England before 1300, and between the two is a single-storey link that houses Gillie's studio. Here she works on semi-figurative oil paintings and makes the colourful, traditional patchwork quilts which she sells and which appear throughout the house. This building is also covered with wooden cladding and, like the other two, roofed in slate. The three enclose a courtyard garden, planted with ebullient greenery. The entire complex fits snugly into the surrounding woods.

The result is a rambling, complicated sort of building with, James says, enormous variety in its spaces and angles. None of the rooms rivals in drama the great expanse of the barn, which is not divided into rooms except for a gallery. Huge braced collar trusses stabilize the whole area, which is designed to show off the skilled carpentry of his firm. There is neither a ceiling nor any attempt to hide the

THIS PAGE AND OPPOSITE
The James family house is very much a working establishment. Roderick James uses it to demonstrate his architectural skills to clients, while Gillie has an artist's studio there – and the entire family spends free time messing about in boats. Brilliantly coloured windcheaters, wellington boots and swimming flippers mingle with old model yachts, rows of storm lanterns and locally found animals' skulls and agricultural implements in the mud room. The whole area is a treasure trove of old maritime equipment, such as ropes and life belts.

beams and braces. The floor is pale wood, as is much of the furniture, while sofas and chairs are covered in plain colours. Natural light pours down from roof lights, and a huge log fire is of near-brutalist concrete with faux tiles painted on by Gillie. Decoy birds and Gillie's paintings are the only decoration.

The couple once made decoys for a living, and made several trips to the East Coast of the USA, where the wooden water birds are so imaginatively carved. The influence of the maritime East Coast states, whether in their home's construction, its colouring or the use of light, is evident throughout.

A scale model of a typical timber frame stands on a table beside the building's front door in an area which acts as both an office and reception area for clients and the dining area of the barn. Its timbered walls are infilled not with wattle and daub but with great slabs of glass which give enormous sweeping views across the garden to the quiet creek beyond.

Of course, the whole point of the complex design is to emphasize these views over the water and woods. This is why the wide, balustraded balcony

provides wide vistas from the bedrooms of visitors and the family alike. Nearly 2.5 metres (8 ft) above the ground, it runs round the entire area of the original house and every bedroom opens onto it. People can walk all around it, taking in the generous southern English scenery. The rooms' French windows are glazed and painted a soft sea blue, and there are comfortable wooden American chairs for lounging during open-air summer breakfasts and siestas (yes, even in Devon). In winter the same walkway offers the chance to spot migrant shore birds arriving from the sea. Similar chairs turn up in the garden and on the verandah under the balustrade, which is, of course, protected from the rain.

Among the 45 projects Roderick James has on the go at the moment, ten are for waterside houses, with which he feels a real affinity. 'Everyone loves living by the waterside; people are drawn to it because it is fundamental to life. Once you come to live by the water, you'll never go away.' At Seagull House, the creek provides constant variety, if variety can ever be constant. 'The feeling of the

ABOVE LEFT **One of the first things that Roderick James did to his dull building was to give it ground-floor verandahs and upper-floor balconies. Clapboard walls have been painted a muted American red, and – equally influenced by East Coast style – Adirondack chairs stand on the decking.**

LEFT The main living room resembles the inside of a boat's upturned hull. It is constructed with timber framing – a craft pioneered in England 700 years ago and now enjoying a revival. The whole room serves as a reminder of James's love affair with timber.

THIS PAGE The glass walls of the dining area would, in medieval times, have been filled with wattle and daub. In the 21st century glass gives far more light and accentuates the views. Canvas buckets, binoculars and old yachts are found in every corner.

water is ever-changing because it's tidal. One minute the whole area can be just mud with shorebirds, and later it all fills with water.'

Here and in his waterside houses designed for clients, James is always conscious of the location, be it by the sea, an estuary or a river. He likes to give each its own sophisticated nautical feeling, alluding to the rigging of boats, to jetties and balconies. 'We use whatever is appropriate, such as granite tiles or oak timbering. I've created one waterside home with a curved double-turf roof.' Everywhere he tries to maximize the peculiar light,

'Everyone loves living by the water; people are drawn to it because it is fundamental to life. Once you come to live by the water, you'll never go away.'

THE WAY THE WOOD IS USED RECALLS MARITIME BUILDINGS AND SHIPS' CABINS. BEDROOMS AND BATHROOMS ARE PANELLED WITH ROUGHLY SAWN PLANKS RUNNING HORIZONTALLY, AND THE JOINTS ARE FILLED WITH A PAINTER'S CAULK OF SOFT WHITE.

shadows and ripple effect that come from moving water. He calls it 'glintering'. 'It's important to get the angles and positions right for the sun, the water and the roofs to ensure that light bounced off the water reflects on the ceilings.'

In Seagull House you will find model yachts in bathrooms and bedrooms and given prime position at the end of the dining room. There are decoy birds everywhere, too – wild ducks, geese, and shorebirds like snipe and sandling. The Jameses even made their own metal cut-out curlew stick-up decoys which are driven into the mud of the creek with integral poles. 'We know they work because the day after we set up 13 of them each had a seagull on its head!'

The way the wood is used inside also recalls maritime buildings and ships' cabins. Bedrooms and bathrooms are panelled with planks which, unusually, run horizontally rather than in vertical lines. The planks are roughly sawn and the joints filled with a painter's

caulk of soft white. Gillie's studio, by contrast, is painted white throughout – floor, walls, ceiling – allowing the strong colours of her paintings and quilts to provide the interest.

James is very proud of his nautical blood, which may explain why he feels so at home working with wood and water. 'My forebears were sea captains, the owners of barques, schooners, brigantines. I have a genetic link with the sea, and I have always had boats.' He has them still – no fewer than six can be seen from Seagull House, moored across the creek. The house's mud room is filled with the primary shades of oilskins and slickers, sea boots and flippers, jammed in with more model yachts and hurricane lanterns. There are dozens of lanterns, which come out to welcome and light the way to the house for parties on dark nights. It is a practice utterly in keeping with the waterside setting, where lights have been used for centuries to guide and cheer travellers, fishermen and sailors.

THIS PAGE AND OPPOSITE An enormous 19th-century family portrait turned out to be just the right size to fit, floor to ceiling, in this inviting guest bedroom. The simple iron bed, painted white, is covered in one of Gillie's pretty quilts, whose sandy colours with splashes of blue pick up the muted decorative theme of the rest of the room. The walls resemble those of a log cabin. They are boarded horizontally, and the gaps are filled with marine caulk Above the head of the bed are a couple of the family's old model yachts – collectors' items that are now almost impossible to find.

a boat-lover's island paradise

Rowing, sailing and fishing are the favourite pastimes on this secluded island that remains largely native bush.

The architect Terry Dorrough, like Les Reedman (see pages 88–93), lives on Dangar Island on the Hawkesbury river near Sydney. Until the middle of the 19th century the island was used by Australian aboriginal people, as evidenced by the rock art and shell middens scattered around the place.

But in the 1780s, says Dorrough, 'The governor of Australia came with his crew to explore the river and camped on the island, calling it Mullet Island. In 1864 the island was bought from the Crown by the Dangar family, who in the 1880s built a large holiday home there as a retreat from their home in Sydney.

'The Dangar house was used as a guest house until it burned down in 1939. Very little of the original house now remains, apart from a stone tower and an old boatshed.' What the Dangars were doing in the 1880s, other Sydney folk were doing in the 1980s, so

today there are about 200 homes on the island, owned either by people who live there full-time or by those who live and work in Sydney but travel across to the island by boat for relaxed weekends.

'We lived for a year in the small boatshed/cottage on the waterfront while planning the new house. This gave us time to experience the site in different seasons and at different times of the day and night,' explains Dorrough, who runs his architectural practice from home. 'I had become involved in a community-funded management plan for the island, aimed at preserving its unique character, and helped to persuade the local Hornsby Council to adopt a strong development-control plan. Our aim was to fit into the context of timber-and-fibro weekenders, boatsheds and jetties. We were not interested in fashion or style but in a house that really worked as a place to live.'

Terry Dorrough, an architect, has been deeply involved in the development of historic Dangar Island and its busy waterways. His house is carefully positioned to take advantage of the trees and shrubs on the slopes, and its cheerful yellow walls are perfectly coloured to catch leafy shadows. He was keen that it should look inviting from the water at night – and the night-time view of the water was important too.

THIS PAGE AND OPPOSITE   The secret of Dorrough's success has been to make the interior and the exterior of the house interchangeable. Verandahs and decking are used to bring the sunshine and views into the rooms – which are protected from too much heat by overhanging roofs – while more decking and corrugated-iron roofs link the various parts of the building, which has been constructed on three different levels. It is particularly satisfying to create something stylish from vernacular materials. The surrounding bush is full of birds such as the white cockatoo shown on the opposite page.

The new house steps up the slope on three levels, carefully sited to preserve existing trees and maximize access to sunlight and views. Its main living area has a strong post-and-beam timber frame, which contrasts with the coloured aluminium sliding and pivoting doors. The doors can be thrown open for most of the year to transform the living, kitchen and verandah areas into one high, flowing space. Beyond the stone fireplace, the bedroom and shower open onto a screened porch, which invites in filtered morning sun and evening moonlight.

The colours — muted warm greys, yellows and off-whites, and cooler purple greys — were inspired by the seasonal changes in the trunks of the surrounding Blackbutt trees. 'Seen from the river, the wide gable of the verandah/living area echoes, on a larger scale, the

existing cottage/boatshed,' explains Dorrough. 'The north-facing waterfront site, sheltered from southerlies and winter westerlies, has a fairly ideal microclimate. The house is flooded with sun in winter, thanks to the high gable roof, north-facing glazing and ridge skylight. The open fire provides enough heating for the living area, and its central location helps to warm the bedroom. For us, the finished house is a spacious, workable and stimulating living environment, built on a difficult site for a very modest cost.'

Costing cannot have been easy, for Dangar Island is, like Venice, surrounded by sea and not suited to cars. 'There is no vehicular access to the island, except by barge for the transport of materials. The roads, though formed, are essentially for pedestrian and wheelbarrow traffic.'

Translate that into the fact that every single necessity for the new house arrived by barge and was taken to the site thereafter by wheelbarrow. 'We acted as owner-builders in order to keep control of costs and allow for experiment and change as the work progressed. We were fortunate to have skilled local carpenters who built the house to a "lock-up" stage while we, over time, completed the finishes, built-in joinery and so on.'

The house was planned around a series of outdoor sitting, dining and working spaces, to take advantage of different aspects of the site and for use in different seasons or at different times of day. On the main axis from the water, a waterfront working deck extends out from the boatshed, and a roof deck – a place to relax near the water – has been built over the boatshed. On the main level is a large covered outdoor room for year-round living, while the courtyard deck on the middle level is a sheltered sun trap. The grassy terrace above the house is tree-shaded and cool in summer, and immediately below the house is a moon-viewing terrace with barbecue. On the

A boathouse has been built at the water's edge so that the owners can sunbathe as well as come and go over the water and explore the creeks and inlets all around. Much reference is made to the sea and the area's maritime past, with driftwood painted like a fish, rusty anchors, and shells chosen to reflect the colours used in the house. The house's airy rooms are often toplit as well as getting light from the large windows. The natural wood floors extend, without a break, to the open verandahs and the view beyond. Hardly any colours obtrude – all the furniture and décor are left natural.

cross axis there is an additional western deck to let winter sun flow into the dining area, and an eastern screen porch for filtered morning sun and evening moonlight to shine into the bedroom and shower.

A lot of the island is still native bush, and the 200-odd home owners are determined to keep it that way. Because the island is quite small there are no large animals such as kangaroo, but there are lots of birds, some of them quite demanding. 'Kookaburras, magpies, currawongs and rainbow lorikeets regularly land on the verandah rail, demanding in raucous voices to be fed. The lorikeets screech like small parrots and are very colourful. Possums clamber over the roof and make quite a noise, too.'

A major pleasure for everyone is boating. 'Boating and fishing are, of course, common pastimes on the island. Most people have a "tinny" – an aluminium boat with outboard motor that is used for commuting. Rowing is popular. There is an annual round-the-island rowing race at Easter. I also have a small yacht and sail regularly in the nearby waterways.'

Like everyone who lives beside the water, Terry Dorrough is captivated by the constant change it offers. 'It's like living in the mountains. You get a wider view. Somehow, nature is always there but different every day. We are tidal so the river is never static, and at night there's the moon or stars shining on the water.

'I think being by the water exaggerates everything. When it's calm, it's very calm, and when there are storms you get the worst of it. You are very aware of the weather – unlike living in the bush or the suburbs. We are well attuned to the island because we have to deal with it every day. We come and go, using the boat, at high and low tide. Sydney is only 10 minutes away in the boat, then a train journey of an hour into the centre. But you can come back at night when the weather is filthy, nasty.'

Dorrough owns a small fleet of boats: 'A runabout with an outboard, a small sailing boat and a racing yacht. Mostly we take the yacht for a day's sailing but we can spend a night away on it. There are so many places to sail, intricate ins and outs. We don't have to go to the ocean. All around here is national park, protected. I have been sailing since I was a boy and have always loved the water and boats. I introduced my wife to sailing when we were first married and, although she is not madly keen, she accepts a boat-orientated life.' I know the feeling exactly.

the sights of Sydney

A penthouse on Sydney Harbour's north shore combines some of the world's most spectacular city views with the solitude and peace that come from its location near a waterfront reserve.

I find the story of Peter and his wife Tonia quite extraordinary. Australians, one of Italian descent and the other with a Russo-Greek background, and both over 60, they were happy to change their lives radically when their two children grew up and they found – purely by accident – the home of their dreams.

Indeed, their apartment on Cremorne Point on the shores of Sydney Harbour must be the place of most people's dreams. Like Big Ben and the Eiffel Tower, the Sydney Opera House with its six leaning triangles is unmistakable. The Harbour Bridge has one of the most famous profiles on the globe – even more than London's Tower

Bridge or San Francisco's Golden Gate. And this is the view that greets Peter and Tonia every morning. They eat breakfast with it as a backdrop; later they sit in the darkening evening with the harbour lights and the city lighting up like a Christmas tree around them every night. They see it in brilliant winter sunshine, when colours in Sydney are even brighter than in spring or summer because the haze disappears and you can see clearly for vast distances.

It is extraordinary that it all happened by accident. Twelve years ago Peter and Tonia were living in a 'Federation' house in Sydney's suburbs, something of roughly the same period as Britain's Arts and

THIS PAGE AND OPPOSITE
The vista is world famous. On the left is Sydney Opera House, designed by the Danish architect Jorn Utzon, which opened in 1973. The Harbour Bridge – more than 1,000 metres (3,000 ft) long and opened in 1932 – is silhouetted on the right. It is this busy stretch of water that Peter and Tonia overlook each day, and celebrate every night as the sun goes down.

Crafts Movement. They had bought it as an ancient relic, with electricity that could be used for little more than summoning the servants and no plumbing in the kitchen. On a larger than average allotment of land, it had generous gardens all around. At the same time Peter's extended family of brothers had a 'hobby farm' 80 minutes' drive away on McMasters Beach. Here they played at repairing fences and raising cattle, learning to ride and teaching horses to jump.

Then Peter and Tonia heard that developers of a building on Cremorne Point were looking for an investor to buy into the new property. Since their two children were growing up and would soon leave home, they knew they needed less space. 'We wanted something that would give us more freedom and convenience and yet still offer the pleasures of the peace and quiet of the garden suburb.'

Their new home is a penthouse at the top of a terraced building on a long, narrow promontory jutting into Sydney Harbour on the north shore. 'The location is perfect. We own a boat and have a mooring close by which we can see from the apartment. Cremorne Point is not far from the Heads and the open sea and yet close to the city. A day's boating gets us up the estuaries of the Parramatta and Lane Cove rivers and Middle Harbour. We are near the yacht club in Mosman Bay. We like going to the theatre and dining out, and the Opera House and city centre are only 10 minutes away by ferry. We rarely use the car.'

The living room, study, terrace and kitchen look across the shipping lanes of the main harbour to the central business district. Cremorne Point has some of the best views in the city – a panorama from north Sydney across Milson's Point, the Harbour Bridge, city skyscrapers, the Opera House, the Royal Botanic Gardens, along with Fort Denison (a little island fort built in the 1850s), Garden Island, the dockyards and Rushcutters Bay – the base for the recent Olympic yachting events. To the north-east are Bradley's Head

THIS PAGE AND OPPOSITE

Everything in this Sydney apartment is subordinated to the view over the harbour – and many of the architectural features also recall the water. In the main living room off-white sofas and a coved ceiling resembling that of a liner are all directed at the

telescope which stands looking out at the Harbour Bridge. Blue-painted chairs are lined up beside a white-clothed table ready for breakfast beside a vista overlooking Sydney Opera House, while a simple wooden floor is planked in the direction of the view.

firework displays right in front of us, and, because we are so high up and have such long views, the cloud formations and weather patterns, sunrises and sunsets are quite fantastic.'

The new house has literally changed their lives. Where once they farmed and gardened for fun, now Peter has become a yachtsman. With money he had saved to build a house on the farm he has bought a Beneteau Oceanis 430 yacht. 'I soon discovered that the Sydney Amateur Sailing Club (the oldest yacht club in Sydney) was nestling in the bush foreshore at Mosman Bay. I decided to buy a boat and take up sailing.' So he learned about seamanship, navigation, radio operating and meteorology, and set off in the boat. 'A comfortable day's sailing up the coast is Broken Bay, where there's an immense area of protected water – a national park – the size of Sydney Harbour. You can get lost there for a couple of weeks.'

and the wharf at the Taronga Zoological Gardens. 'Our bedrooms face the east side of the promontory, and when we wake up in the mornings we enjoy the sun and another water view, of Athol Bay and Bradley's Head. We're six levels up from the street.'

As if that weren't enough, the whole of Cremorne Point is bordered by the Cremorne Waterfront Reserve with its scenic walks and formal gardens interspersed with native Australian bush. 'It's very quiet and feels remote from the city, with lorikeets, cockatoos and kookaburras among the trees. At night boats ply up and down – tourist cruiseboats, ferries and large ocean-going ships constantly on the move. And the Harbour Bridge, Opera House, Fort Denison, docks and city are all brilliantly lit. There are often

Instead of gardening, he potters with the planters on the penthouse's terrace, where he grows orchids, bougainvillea, petunias and pansies. Once a month, if he feels like doing more gardening, he can join in the Foreshore Garden and Bush Regeneration Group. 'We do three or four hours' work, then have a leisurely picnic lunch. You know, we would never give it up. We love it so much.'

THE PROMONTORY IS BORDERED BY A WATERFRONT NATURE RESERVE WHERE SCENIC WALKS AND FORMAL GARDENS ARE INTERSPERSED WITH NATIVE AUSTRALIAN BUSH.

Australian dream time

Tranquillity and solitude are life's main features on the banks of a 'drowned valley'.

There's waterside living and there's living on an island, which is something entirely different. A house at the waterside is at a dead end. Instead of a circumference of places to go from home, you have only 180° worth, unless you are intrepid enough to take to the water in a boat. Living on an island is a choice in isolation. You are not necessarily cut off from the rest of the world, but you are very much part of a chosen community. Island dwellers somehow feel as though they were living in a remote village in the mountains. You know everyone and they know you; the only way to enjoy the life is to make sure that you fit in. If you don't, woe betide you.

Dangar Island in Australia features twice in this book (Terry Dorrough's home is on pages 78–83) because it obviously attracts people who are looking for that quality of remoteness and isolation found on islands and yet, at the same time, for surroundings which can be quickly changed, for Sydney is just around the corner.

THIS PAGE AND OPPOSITE
Les Reedman, an architect, found an abandoned fisherman's shack on the shores of Dangar Island. Rather than demolish and rebuild, he wove his house in and out of the old building, keeping all its character. A major change was to add a wide verandah, which **takes full advantage of the view and the busy shipping lanes beyond. All around the building are places to sit for meals, for relaxation and for river viewing. Most of the islanders have boats – not just for hobby sailing, but to travel to meet friends and even to go to work in nearby Sydney.**

Les Reedman, who is both a chartered architect and an architectural historian, managed to combine the life of an islander with a busy architectural practice in Sydney itself. 'My house was my weekend retreat from the city. It's on an island near the outlet of a broad east-coast river, the Hawkesbury. The island's beach, which the house overlooks, was visited by officers of the British First Fleet within weeks of their arrival in 1788 at Port Jackson farther south.'

The house is now his full-time home and Sydney is simply visited from time to time. 'My house is a modest two-bedroom "cabin" with a full-width verandah facing east across the river to the sandstone cliffs. The construction is lightweight timber framing clad mainly with glass in timber frames. It's a practical construction for a dwelling across a waterway in a temperate climate: most rooms get a view.' His drawings for the house show at least six areas for beds, and other parts are designated 'Dream', 'Write', 'Relax', 'Potter' and 'Cook', while at the edge of the building are designated water views, fishing and swimming areas and steep steps which lead to the forest at the back of the house.

'When I bought the land in 1970 it had a dilapidated fibro-clad fisherman's shack built after World War Two from this and that. It had two small rooms and a tiny verandah with lots of fish drawings on the wall. I kept the core rooms and built a surrounding lightweight structure providing a generous verandah and bathroom, sleepout, laundry and kitchen – all with views.'

The Hawkesbury river is wide and interesting, with wooded banks interspersed with cliffs rolling up at each side. 'The verandah has extensive views over the river to the sandstone cliffs which glow in the afternoon sun. There are hundreds of Aboriginal rock carvings on the hills all round the river, evidence of an earlier habitation.'

So, while the area appears to have a history which dates back to the 1780s and the first white settlers, in fact it spirals back into the past and into prehistory itself. 'The estuary is a "drowned valley" after the rise of the sea tens of thousands of years ago. The river catchment is very extensive, draining a high rainfall from as far south as inland Goulburn and up to the Great Dividing Coastal Range in the west. The river has worn its way in time through sandstone which has resulted in many figured cliffs and sculptured rock outcrops, hundreds of feet high, from the Blue Mountains to the sea.

'There is much evidence that the Dharug Aboriginal tribe lived in the area before white settlement. There are many shell middens on salient points around the river, and there are the rock carvings on elevated flat-rock areas which command water views important in their ceremonies. The carvings show the outlines mainly of fish, snakes and wallabies – wildlife which can be still seen today but much diminished by encroaching development.'

The modern primitive drawings of fish which Les Reedman has so cleverly kept on the walls of his converted home make a parallel with these ancient carvings, and, he says, the birdlife around is still plentiful and what the aboriginals would have known – kookaburras, sea eagles, whistling kites and pelicans, all birds of the sea.

'The first houses on the island were built for workers of the Brooklyn Bridge Company which built the nearby main Northern Rail Bridge across the Hawkesbury in the 1880s, which completed the rail link from Sydney to the north. The bridge was opened in 1889 by Sir Henry Parker, the New South Wales premier, who noted that it was a first step to the Federation of Australian states. Ten years later the drafting party of the Federation spent a weekend on a steamboat here, no doubt to conclude the constitution.'

THE ESTUARY IS BOTH WILD AND TIDAL THOUGH NOT AS FIERCE AT THE OCEAN BEYOND. ISLANDERS LIKE LES REEDMAN ARE CONSTANTLY EXPLORING ITS CHANNELS, FISHING LIKE THE OWNERS OF THE ORIGINAL CABIN, AND ENJOYING THE FULL SCOPE OF ISLAND LIFE.

OPPOSITE PAGE   A bright yellow kitchen cabinet with stained-glass doors houses a collection of teapots, while kitchen equipment is deliberately hung to be silhouetted against a window. Feathers found around the island and pictures of boats and the sea are all cluttered in.

THIS PAGE   The trick with an unassuming house such as this old fisherman's shack is to allow all the details to blend in. Les Reedman has made little attempt to find grand or over-stylish furniture, using his eye instead to find pieces from the mid 20th century.

Some time in the 1920s living on Dangar Island became desirable. 'The island was subdivided for house lots then and the first river dwellings began to appear. Today there are almost 200 houses, a bowling club, community hall, fire station and shop.'

A ferry service connects the island and river with the mainland Brooklyn township. Rather than rely on the ferry, most inhabitants are happy to sail across from the island to the mainland and then continue by train to Sydney. 'I have a boatshed and a couple of boats,' says Reedman, 'one to cross the channel to the mainland and the other, a bit bigger, to sail around the estuary. I go fishing when I can.'

The estuary is both wild and tidal though not, of course, as fierce at the real ocean beyond. Islanders like Reedman are constantly exploring its channels, fishing like the owners of the original cabin, and enjoying the full scope of island life. To that end the rooms of the house are simple and relaxed. The floors

are of wood, with the wooden frames of the windows also left natural. Feathers are propped against seascapes, and, outside, gum trees lean over almost into the verandah and the huge windows.

The whole building seems as if it is constructed of glass, and if you are lucky enough to sail by on the river below at dusk, as the lights come on, you will catch a glimpse of this impressive building, in character like a giant boat house or barn with its low-pitched roof shining out against the silhouettes of the trees all around.

Despite all the pressures of development, Reedman can still call Dangar Island 'a pristine environment'. The reason is that the residents are 'extremely protective' of their beautiful island which, he says, 'remains heavily timbered with large native eucalyptus, wattles and native flowering shrubs.'

The trouble with writing this book is that, with every case study I write, I wish I was there for ever.

OPPOSITE PAGE One of the most interesting features of the original shack was that the previous occupants – all fishermen – had sketched the varieties and sizes of the local fish on the building's wall – and I bet they used a bit of fishermen's licence.

THIS PAGE The fishermen's artwork has been preserved; Les has added the occasional touch of a deep-brimmed hat (to guard against the insect population) and a book on how to tell what has stung you. Fishermen don't have everything easy. Greedy representatives of the local bird life such as pelicans can get there first.

going Dutch in Paris

This is the story of a snapper-up of unconsidered trifles, a great rummager in flea markets, antique shops and even skips – so it is hardly surprising that his boat was bought by accident too.

Rupert Morgan had decided that property prices in London had gone mad – '£40,000 for a broom cupboard in Knightsbridge. I didn't want a broom cupboard, even in central London' – so a boat seemed to be the answer. He went to a boatyard with something small and cheap in mind and ended up with a 23-metre (75-ft)-long Tjaalk built in 1913. 'The Dutch built boats like these for 400 years, up to the First World War. Mine is one of the last, with steel planks used exactly as wooden planks were in earlier versions. It is 4.3 metres (14 ft) wide and weighs 50 tonnes.' It cost him £58,000, just a bit more than a broom cupboard, but is moored only ten minutes' walk away from the Arc de Triomphe in Paris. When Rupert saw the boat, 'There

Rupert Morgan is a man who can't resist a flea market or an old boat yard – the Dutch Tjaalk which he bought on impulse has led to a life of wandering around the rivers and canals of Europe, calling in at more boatyards and junk shops. The wide deck – no one could claim this is a greyhound among boats – is a handy place for a sunny breakfast. He made the tiny kitchen – 'like a cockpit' – with more pieces found in old shops. The dining-room table is an old haberdasher's advertising sign. Rupert distressed the clock himself.

WHEREVER RUPERT AND KARIN TRAVEL THEY ARE ON THE LOOKOUT FOR ANTIQUES AND JUNK THAT CAN BE ADAPTED TO DIFFERENT USES. RUPERT TENDS TO DO THE FIXING AND CARPENTRY, WHILE IT IS UP TO KARIN TO LOOK AFTER THE COLOURS AND FABRICS.

was sunlight pouring in from every direction, teak parquet flooring, a big living room, three bedrooms and two bathrooms. It had central heating and a wood-burning stove, plus a choice of three forms of electricity: mains, battery or the biggest generator you've ever seen. It had a two-tiered deck, with room for a dining table, deckchairs, a herb garden and an inflatable swimming pool. The only problem was that it might, in rare circumstances, sink.' It was love at first sight.

Bachelor Morgan set sail along canals and rivers and, in extremely calm weather, across stretches of sea. He also gave up his day job in advertising for a novelist's life, and has since published two satires on modern life, *Let There Be Life* and *Something Sacred.*

Then he married half-French Karin and they now have two daughters, four-year-old Jade and one-year-old Nina. The three bedrooms that were made into one when he married have now been converted into two, one for the children, and the teak floor is temporarily covered with seagrass. The *Albatross* (not a fair name for such a useful boat) has become immobile while the children are young, and the Morgans have also bought a home in the depths of the French countryside. But it's hard to imagine that they will ever part with their boat.

Rupert becomes lyrical when talking about the advantages of living on water. 'There is something about living on a boat which is not normal life. One enters an entirely different world. We're moored in the middle of Paris but there are ducks, swans and turtles swimming past.' Turtles? Yes, really. 'And it's quite open. The reason I bought the boat was simply economic – it was all I could afford – but, apart from those people who get discouraged, everyone who tries it catches the bug. Boating is like luxury camping: you're aware of the weather, you hear the rain falling – there's a great feeling of liberty. It's wonderful to pull up anchor and take your home with you.

'Travelling in your own boat causes zero stress. You are not wrecking the countryside. It is just that the unspoiled places cannot be reached by car. I know hundreds of idyllic spots, some of them just outside towns, where nothing has changed in a hundred years. But you can only get there by water.'

Rupert is adept at carpentry. 'Most things on a boat needs to be built in because the walls are not straight, but we have tried to make everything look as though it was always there.' What was already there was the wheelhouse with steps leading to a two-level saloon with its inbuilt curved wooden sofa. The sturdy bathroom and shower were also already there in 1913 but the Morgans created the minuscule kitchen – about 3 square metres (32 square ft). 'It's like a cockpit,' Rupert says. 'Everything is within reach, and we can make really good meals in there.'

But there is a downside. 'All the things we take for granted on dry land are operated by individual machines: drinking-water pump, waste-water pump, electric lavatories. They can go wrong.'

Indeed, they go wrong so often that the Morgans are now expert at fixing them. 'It's deeply unpleasant work, make no mistake – for some reason it always involves sticking your head into some rank-smelling greasy recess with a torch in your mouth.'

But it makes no difference to their love of the boat. Even trips to London are heavenly. 'When you're on the river, London is a beautiful town, with clean air and magnificent sunsets.'

THIS PAGE AND OPPOSITE:
Morgan began his wandering life as a bachelor but later married Karin and began a family. Karin is responsible for the choice of fabrics such as the jolly shower curtain. The walls behind the bath are papered with quantities of old advertisements from a 1920s lifestyle magazine, while the mirror belonged to Karin's grandparents. Karin also took some excerpts from Rupert's unpublished novel to print on the duvet cover. The brass lamps found everywhere on the boat are old stage footlights, while Le Parfait jars are used for storing pasta. Even the books – 1960s Penguins – are old.

'There is something about living on a boat which is not normal life. One enters a different world. We're moored in the middle of Paris but there are ducks, swans and turtles swimming past.'

a houseboat on the Seine

Its style reflects the sophisticated Parisian view of a French cottage.

Home for one former designer is a houseboat moored on the River Seine only a short distance from the centre of Paris with, as she says, its stinks and traffic jams. Rectangular and far from aerodynamic, the boat looks as though it was never intended to move from the banks – and this sensation is increased by the unnautical arrangement of evergreens and bamboos in pots among the ropes on deck, and by the wooden deck chairs and parasols that would provoke the average stout seadog to intemperate protests about clutter.

It is, somehow, a very French houseboat. Half is given over to a two-storey section where the less ornate rooms – a ground-floor main bedroom and bathroom, a kitchen plus two more bedrooms up a narrow stairway – are housed. The rest is half-open deck with, below it, an all-white living room where comfortable sofas and chairs face out onto the fast-flowing river below. 'My decorator and I decided to use simple, natural fabrics and décor in this area. We put in a whitened wooden floor and lots of woven willow, sisal and natural linen.' From the sunny deck above or, on cold winter days, behind the huge glass windows of the salon, the owner becomes

Houseboats traditionally have plenty of wide flat decks, and here they are used to full advantage for a thriving garden. Bamboos, bays, and other shrubs chosen for their interesting foliage are planted in pots, so that the boat blends in with the banks of the river beyond. Perhaps this encourages the wildlife – mallards are regular visitors to the boat, while swans slide past its bows. The main living space was adapted to have huge plate-glass windows facing onto the river. The gangway (handy for parking the bike) leads into the two-storey section with its iron spiral stairs.

IT IS, SOMEHOW, A VERY FRENCH HOUSEBOAT. FROM THE SUNNY DECK ABOVE OR,
ON COLD WINTER DAYS, BEHIND THE HUGE GLASS WINDOWS OF THE SALON, THE
OWNER BECOMES PART OF THE BUSY LIFE OF PARIS'S GREAT RIVER: THE GNARLED

part of the busy life of Paris's great river: the gnarled fishermen with lines and berets hoping to catch supper, the river traffic of working barges, and the wildfowl that fly in to land nearby. Mallards often appear on deck, and their quacking serves as an early-morning call. 'I just love it here, the nature and the ducks. It's a perfect place to live. I would never leave it.'

Before 1989, when her love affair with the boat hit her like a bolt from the blue, the owner was the chic-est of Parisiennes living among Haussmann's dignified boulevardes and working with a designer. When she moved, her friends thought she had lost the plot. 'They thought I'd gone off my head – that is, until summer came, when they started to applaud what I'd done. Then they even came round to thinking that they should do the same.

'It was an absolute *coup de foudre* when I saw the houseboat. She was ancient, *moche* and far too small. The *coque* was in a pitiable state. But at least one thing really pleased me – I knew that, without any kind of motor, she would never set sail.'

When she had succumbed to her love affair, she called in her friend and decorator Julie Prisca to help to repair and modernize the boat. 'Her help was essential.'

The result is an interior that pays virtually no attention to the houseboat's situation other than to celebrate the marvellous views virtually at water level. You won't find any nauticalia here, except some rather nice oil paintings of the sort of rough seas the old boat will, the owner hopes, never encounter. Instead there are Victorian portraits of a stern couple, given to her by her parents, contrasting with languorous nudes in

FISHERMEN WITH LINES AND BERETS HOPING TO CATCH SUPPER, THE RIVER TRAFFIC OF WORKING BARGES, AND THE WILDFOWL THAT FLY IN TO LAND NEARBY. MALLARDS OFTEN APPEAR ON DECK, AND THEIR QUACKING SERVES AS AN EARLY-MORNING CALL.

THIS PAGE AND OPPOSITE **Nothing in the décor detracts from the fact that the houseboat has splendid views of the outskirts of Paris. Muted wooden chairs and tables sit on bleached decking, a perfect pink rose stands out against a tarpaulin, while even a bowl of cherries plays a part. The whole is surrounded by pots of leafy shrubs. What a place for a sunny breakfast. The main living room in the boat's single-storey section is all white, from sofas to Roman blinds. Huge windows look out over the river, but, apart from the view, this living room could be in a Parisian apartment.**

the blue-and-white bedroom where the bed linen and heaped cushions match the striped wallpaper. Taking the illusion yet further, the ceiling seems to have cottage beams.

Every corner has charming little bouquets of scented flowers, pink roses and cottagey bunches, teamed with small table lights. There are shelves full of elegant books with, above, the owner's collection of ornamental hands – iron paperweights, bits taken from artists' wooden models or from wooden statues. Julie Prisca provided table sculptures made of decorative dried leaves, carefully placed among oriental bowls and small woven baskets.

The dining area also overlooks the river – a small table surrounded by ironwork chairs and, of course, more bunches of flowers. The whole is turned outwards, towards the busy Seine and the green banks of Paris beyond. A plain gangplank, covered in bright green, with rails handy for parking the bike, leads to the shore, which seems a million miles away.

The owner and her decorator have cleverly managed to bring a sophisticated Parisian view of a French cottage onto a houseboat. Everything is extremely comfortable and light, helped by the use of white throughout. The beamed ceilings are white, as is the spiral staircase which leads from inside the front door to the upstairs of the boat. Apart from the bedroom, the walls are a matte white, as are the heavy Roman blinds and cushions in the elegant living room. There is little clutter, with each small painting, gilded hand or antique sculptured head used to maximum effect – it's no surprise to learn that the owner hopes soon to open her own *brocante* shop full of sophisticated finds.

clifftop living

A house perched on a clifftop must have the most exciting of all waterside positions. True, the location may not have the same romance as a sandy beach, but instead it has wide panoramas and big skies. Its storms can be dramatic and its sunsets moving. Clifftoppers revel in theatrical effects.

As well as being generous, vivacious and open-minded people, the Australians Robert and Gabby Reeves are deeply involved in cooking and entertaining. Their architect, Peter Stutchbury, built them a house on Pittwater that mirrors all these characteristics. It is flexible, light-hearted and designed for social cooks. It also takes full advantage of its clifftop position with avant-garde panache.

Philip Cox gave himself an extraordinarily complex brief when he designed and built his own home on Whale Beach near Sydney – but, since he is one of Australia's most influential architects, this was to be expected.

Cox's home had to welcome the family yet entertain a hundred people; it had to be a bolt-hole and yet work as a statement of his own design beliefs. It had to double as an office on occasion. Cox also has managed to keep the building subordinate to the landscape while taking full advantage of the heart-tugging location – a whale even gave birth as he watched the seas below.

The clifftop house in Brittany is as French as the Tricolour. Imagine a warm Mediterranean afternoon (it gets that balmy) where elegant families relax on daybeds with cushions that match the view. Later they will take drinks and a meal thought out with care the day before, while the children play on a beach below. It's like an Impressionist painting with added sounds and scents.

It must be strange to live in a national monument, but that's what happend to Bill and his family after he found, by accident, a lighthouse and its keeper's cottage on the rugged coast of Maine. The building had been immortalized in a painting by Edward Hopper, and the problem was to keep the memorable image while making it large enough for a family home. It has true clifftop glamour: busy shipping on the waves below, migrating birds in season, and the lighthouse beam winking in sequence with others along the coast.

The house owned by an English couple at St James in Barbados is perched on a small cliff, but the site has none of the harsh excitement that one expects from living on the sharp edge. Landscaped gardens full of tropical flowers flow gently down from the house towards a small gate. From here another path descends to a soft sandy beach, protected by coral reefs and edged with palms. A case of the best of all scenarios, I'd say.

in harmony with nature

Built to take advantage of the constantly changing patterns of the water and the movements of the sun, moon and stars, this is a house that seems to float on the land.

If we could produce a wish-list for the perfect waterside house, it would be somewhere we could live at ease surrounded by nature – a house that took full advantage of the views, the constantly changing pattern of water, the movements of the sun, moon and stars. It would be a house so flexible that we could enjoy it privately or with friends in every one of its moods: breakfast as the early sun rises over the water; lunch under the shade of trees with cool breezes moving the branches; and evening meals with friends all around watching the sun descend as the stars come out above.

Fantasy? Maybe not, for – remarkably – this seems to be what the architects Peter Stutchbury and Sue Harper have managed to achieve for their clients Robert Reeves and Gabby Hunt, as they then were. The house was built for them before they married – and their wedding was held there. 'We had the wedding two weeks after we moved in,' says Gabby Reeves, 'along with a party for 60 people.'

Their house at Clareville on Pittwater, the most northerly peninsula around Sydney, seems to be part of the landscape, because that is what they asked for. 'The house seems to float on the land,' says Gabby. 'It is very open, with the inside and outside all one space.' The kitchen – state of the art, because she owns a café and Robert is a food and menu consultant – actually juts out onto an open terrace, so the couple can cook out of doors in the summer. 'Robert cooks a lot and so do I. It's a great place for entertaining.'

Clareville may not have appeared so at first. The architects describe the original site as cold, dark and wet. As a result, the living space had to be lifted up to get the best of the view and 'experience the warmth and freedom of beach-house living'. The water around was landscaped to create a magnificent river, which rambles down the valley and back into Pittwater below. The view, however, was always superb since the site is on the north-eastern slope of the

OPPOSITE PAGE **Robert and Gabby Reeves like to eat outdoors whenever the weather is fine. They are both enthusiastic cooks and entertainers, so they decided to have a kitchen that led out onto an open-air area where they could cook and feed guests all summer. The couple were unusual in that they built this house to get married in, and the brief was that it would be suitable for all kinds of entertaining. Their architect was also asked to make the rooms indoors and outside virtually indistinguishable.**

THIS PAGE **The lush vegetation around the house has been made a prominent feature of the property – large windows right up to the roof mean that the treetops are incorporated into the décor. The whole building is the result of a happy marriage between enterprising clients and a clever architect.**

beach amphitheatre looking out to Pittwater itself. Superb, too, were Stutchbury's clients, described by him as 'a magnificent couple, full of life, exuberance and generosity – welcoming, entertaining, vivacious, free, practical, open-minded, experimental, direct, no fuss'. Such paragons got the best that the architects could produce: a simple but ingenious building that is at once tranquil, transparent and stylish.

It is on several sloping levels, with the private part of the house, for sleeping and seclusion, underneath. This area also adds the necessary height to the main floors and terraces where all the fun happens. The main area is designed to be completely adaptable, which means using the latest technology in a way that is both simple and complex. The lighting, for instance, is generally hidden – recessed into the tops of walls or

inside cavities and under benches. This means that it is very adaptable. Heating is equally clever, with a solid concrete floor and concrete walls that heat up during the day in winter and give out heat at night. In summer the floors and walls act as coolers, while the roof is inclined up to the north and down to the west to encourage sunlight to flood in in winter and stay out in summer. The steel-framed doors and windows are bolted in place, so they can be dismantled and put elsewhere. There are many terraces around the house, making it seem part of the environment; meals can be taken where the view is best at any one time. And the landscaping, by Phoebe Pape, ensures that the trees and flora all around Clareville are part of the design. 'We have had kookaburras come into the house, in one door and out the next. We've had them sitting on the backs of chairs, watching us and joining in by tucking into the oysters when we've had oysters and champagne at lunch. There are also lorikeets, galahs and cockatoos all around us.'

The idea for the house came to them when they decided to have a family. 'We moved here because it would be right for children. We wanted to be near water, and there's a little beach – perfect for picnics.' Their first child, Ruby, was born in October 2000.

'It was a damp 1940s house before, and we spent a lot of time getting the feel for the place. It was in a gulley, but it's now all lifted up.' All around are native spotted gum trees and lemon-scented gums, some of which had to be cut down when the house was built. But the Reeveses have planted 20 more of the fast-growing trees to surround them. 'They are growing really well. The light is now fantastic at any time of the day. The trees start as silhouettes, and at the end of the day we see the sunsets.'

The pair do a lot of kayaking, as well as wandering along the beaches collecting shells and paddling in the pools, when they aren't entertaining friends. 'It's like being on holiday the whole time.'

THIS PAGE AND OPPOSITE Philip Cox's own home on the shores of Whale Beach reflects his concern to keep buildings in touch with their roots and the landscape. From his bedroom there is a clear view of the distinctive humpy headland after which Whale Beach was named.

Real whales also appear in these waters from time to time. A row of casual but comfortable director's chairs have been positioned around the verandah to allow observers to catch all the action that goes on – once a whale gave birth to a calf outside the windows.

enhancing an exotic landscape

In a wild and sensuous setting overlooking the Pacific Ocean, one of Australia's most influential architects has created for himself a weekend home of timber and stone, carved on three levels into the side of a cliff.

Philip Cox is an important Australian architect who works mostly on mega-projects – which is sad for adventurous Australian home-owners because, as his own weekend home demonstrates, his domestic work is at once beautiful, clever, subtle and understated.

The house on Whale Beach amply demonstrates his philosophy: 'When designing houses for other people, which I don't do very often because I'm working on large-scale projects, I consider the landscape the most important feature, having regard to the client's brief. I believe in the philosophy of *genius loci* – if the architecture is correct, it's an enhancement of the landscape.'

In the case of Whale Beach, Cox was, of course, his own client – and he gave himself a brief. His aim was to build a comfortable family weekend home where he could entertain up to a hundred people. It also needed to double as a workplace and as a statement of his own design imperatives – in particular, his approach to the use of materials and what the Australian magazine *Vogue Living* described in 1990 as 'his consummate ability to relate a building to its landscape in the most civilized and harmonious way'.

The landscape around Whale Beach is – at least to this non-Australian – exotic, wild and sensuous. The beach is the most northerly in the metropolitan area of Sydney, only 15 km (9 miles) from the city's central business district. Cox uses it as a retreat because he has a townhouse in the city: 'In Australian terms they're called crash pads – one- or two-bedroom apartments on Sydney Harbour.' This one is in part of a major development by the Cox Group on King Street Wharf. Whale Beach could not be more different. 'It is called that because the headland resembles a whale. Within the shore in front of the house we often have whales, especially in September, when they're en route to their summer holiday in the Antarctic. A few years ago we were able to witness one of these beauties giving birth to a whale calf. They are also majestic and are growing in numbers again because of the whale-hunting moratorium.'

His house is perched on cliffs high above the water. 'The house is in a bushland setting of banksia trees and eucalyptus, with panoramic views of the northern coastline and the Hawkesbury river. The view is dominated by a peninsula of sand, known as

Barrenjoey, which has a lighthouse on its rocky outcrop. The house was designed in response to the site, the surrounding landscape, the water, the sun, all those things. Also the view – looking down at the rocks, looking up and down the coast, looking ahead. I wanted to make an interesting space here for an informal living experience.'

The house is designed on three levels: the upper one is a sun deck with entry hall and studio, where Philip Cox works when he is not in Sydney. The middle level has all the main rooms of the house – the living room and dining room, kitchen, library and main bedroom. 'The whole has an expansive feeling of space opening onto spacious verandahs and decks. All the windows and doors are full-height glass, allowing the maximization of the view so, when you are in these spaces, the Pacific blue horizon is always apparent.' The final, bottom level has extra bedrooms for guests, with their own sitting rooms. These, in turn, open onto their own verandahs, and look out on the ocean through a screen of trees.

The house is made from timber and stone and, he says, 'has the appearance of floating lightly across the landscape'. *Vogue Living* agreed: 'The main part of the house is roofed with that characteristic Cox trademark, vaulted white corrugated steel which drifts from one height to another with graceful languor. The top deck is paved with ceramic tiles in the palest of greens (as in Cox's National Maritime Museum) and partly screened from the sun by the curved sweep of a lightweight tensioned fabric stretched over a white steel frame.'

Extraordinarily, this complex structure was built in no time. 'Twelve months from go to whoa,' says Cox. It was added to an existing Bauhaus-type building, but that probably made the construction more time-consuming than building from scratch. 'I used the roof of it and added this and that,' he comments modestly.

No house can be seen from the building, and – because it is surrounded by a nature reserve, and therefore carefully planned – it, in turn, can barely be seen from the beach below.

'There is no garden in the English tradition,' Cox explains. 'The garden is natural bushland of the most extraordinary textures of fallen leaves and branches with pale-pink trunked angophora lanceolate trees, which have the appearance of stark-naked bodies. Hairy candled banksias are the other dominant species, so the total picture is one of an untouched wilderness.' Banksias are named after Sir Joseph Banks, who sailed with Captain Cook in the

'The house was designed in response to the surrounding landscape, the water, the sun, all those things. Also the view – looking down at the rocks, looking up and down the coast, looking ahead. I wanted to make an interesting space here for an informal living experience.'

As in all the best waterside
houses, the interior is
subordinated to the views
outside. Philip Cox's plain
living room with its massive
fireplace and prominent
chimney is coloured all in
neutrals, with picture
windows looking out over
the large verandah. He is
a keen collector of works by
both Aboriginal potters
and Australia's foremost
ceramicists, including Milton
Moon, Peter Rushforth
and Col Levi. The pieces are
positioned for maximum
impact, their shapes
silhouetted against plain
walls or open spaces.

Endeavour in 1768. He collected many specimens of Australian flora, and the pressed banksia flowers remain in the Natural History Museum's collection in London. In this wilderness there are koala bears, possums, lizards and snakes. 'Snakes are particularly dangerous in Australia, but they usually get out of your way on approach. The problem is accidentally stepping on them. There is a haunting beauty in snakes, especially the redbelly black snake and the green-and-brown diamond python. However, we don't have kangaroos as we are too metropolitan.'

The house is, of course, a retreat, but that does not make it a place that encourages somnolence. Cox and his partner, the journalist Janet Hawley, come here to recharge their batteries and those of the five children they have between them – Janet's Sam, Ben and Kim, and Philip's Charlotte and Sophie. This is where they sail, surf and go bushwalking – 'all the things typical Australians like doing'.

'The water is intense Pacific blue, and I can look from the verandah down onto the rock ledges below and the changing colours of the ocean with its reefs and sand beds. For most of the year the Pacific rollers come crashing across the rocks below, so there is enormous dynamism and interest created at the very foot of the house.

'I entertain often here because the environment is very stimulating. The upper level of the house is partially enclosed by a translucent cover so that, throughout the year, we are able to enjoy the temperate climate and a two-way view either of the ocean or the bushland behind.

'Light is a most important part of the design. The roof has glazed strips with controllable louvre systems allowing the penetration of winter sun into the house while excluding summer sun. The result of this is the fascinating shadows and the drama of cloud changes within the house.

'Living in the house is romantic: watching the moon rise over the vast Pacific reflecting the silver reflections across the rippling waves. We watch the sun set over the hills of the nearby national park. The hills turn indigo and the sky a deep orange. The romance of the light is the most intriguing sensation.'

OPPOSITE PAGE **Philip Cox felt that it was crucial for the house to fit naturally into a scene dominated by rampant vegetation. Those windows that don't face the water look out onto vast natural boulders and rockfalls, all with local flora growing among them. The land has not been planted but allowed to go back to nature, as seen from this bathroom window.**

THIS PAGE **Most of the plants have exotic, large foliage, but occasionally brilliant scarlet semi-tropical flowers appear. They grow against huge stone blocks which turn satisfyinging black when wet. Cox also uses the water to create features amid the rocks.**

THE HOUSE IS, OF COURSE, A RETREAT, BUT THAT DOES NOT MAKE IT A PLACE THAT ENCOURAGES SOMNOLENCE. PHILIP COX AND HIS FAMILY COME HERE TO RECHARGE THEIR BATTERIES – THIS IS WHERE THEY SAIL, SURF AND GO BUSHWALKING.

Breton chic on a rocky bluff

This romantic creeper-clad house bathes in the subtle light of France's north-west coast.

The light found around the coasts has always attracted artists. Schools of painters have established themselves at the Cornish seaside resorts of St Ives and Newlyn; painters, poets and musicians were drawn to Naples in the 18th century; in California, David Hockney has found the brilliant light to be an inspiration, as Gauguin did in the South Sea islands.

There are plenty of places along the French coast that have contributed enormously to the way we see things today. Henri Matisse and Raoul Dufy couldn't get enough of the vibrant quality of the Mediterranean light along the Riviera, while late 19th-century artists, including the Impressionists, loved the charms of the north-west coast. We see the pretty ladies in bustles and the handsome gentlemen in moustaches and bowlers promenading around the smart coastal towns of Deauville, Trouville, Le Havre and St Malo.

It is at Manegor, quite close to St Malo, that Laurence Sabouret and her husband, Yves, have decided to spend their holidays and weekends – and it is the light there that inspires them, too. Laurence tells of Picasso's visits to the area and how she delights in walking along the beaches where, a century ago, he walked and got ideas for his paintings.

The northern light along these coasts is more subtle than the bright light of the Mediterranean. The sky is often overcast and cloudy, providing the shadowless effect that artists strive after in their

OSITE Recognizing that the Breton house has a strong
, the owners have disciplined their input. The colours are
tral shades enlivened with bright sea blues, navy and other
living room has blue curtains, blue piped sofas with creamy

covers and cream Roman blinds. During good weather the French windows
are kept open to allow in the salty sea air. Deck loungers are also made with
plain wood and cream fabrics, while the lifebuoys represent an element of
fun rather than a reliable form of life-saving equipment.

north-facing studios. The colours are more subdued and the contrasts less violent, and the overall touch of mist and rain is evocative of days spent walking briskly along the sands, hearing the cries of the seabirds combating the gales, searching for objects washed up among the rollers – and then heading smartly back home to warm fires, hot baths and bowls of steaming soup.

True romantics believe that there is much to be gained from the contrasts of the weather – the brilliance of the morning sun over a calm sea superseded by inky storm clouds whipping up white horses by lunchtime. Anyone who chooses to perch alongside the Atlantic must enjoy being indoors, preferably snuggled in a cashmere throw, as much as they enjoy the clear skies and calm after the storm. And then, of course, there are days as brilliantly blue and calm as anything the Mediterranean can offer, when life is lived on a terrace overlooking blue waters dotted with boats at anchor.

Laurence and Yves, with their children Louis-Benoît, Paul and Victoire, come to Manegor from Paris, experiencing a complete change from sophistication to rurality that provides a welcome relief from the constant stress of the city.

They way they do so is extremely French. Not for them the barbies on the beach and the shorts and flip-flops that characterize Australian waterside living – nor do they follow British ideas of superior camping. While the Americans treat their holiday homes as ideal for outdoor entertaining, the French are not willing to give up formality, the *comme il faut* of daily life. If the holiday home is to be enjoyed, it must be done so with rules.

Built about 100 years ago, the Sabourets' house is, says Laurence, typical of the *balnéaire* architecture found all along the coast – 'inherited from the Normandy example seen at Deauville but with a typically Breton twist. In the salon the walls are covered with oak *boiseries* and there's a large fireplace, also in oak, carved with Breton motifs.' The building's high and spiky roof is covered in steely slates, with large red chimneys poking up and through. Like much architecture of the period the house is asymmetric, but an all-covering creeper brings the whole together. The windows have charming French louvred shutters which are clearly intended to be used, against both the hot sun during the summer days and the storm-force winds that howl around in winter.

The house stands high up on a rocky bluff softened by quantities of evergreen and deciduous native trees, and the whole property has a distinctive silhouette when seen from the water below.

The view from the terrace is stupendous: framed by the branches of pines and the rocky outcrops is the sea, dotted in summer with scores of yachts. During the day the scene is almost unreal in its beauty – think of a particularly idyllic film set – while at night, one by one, the lights of the boats flicker on.

Laurence Sabouret has been extremely clever in bringing the scene below into the décor of the house above. She has not been tempted to paint over the heavy colour of the oak panelling, whose arched fields are repeated both in the large doors themselves and in the arches above the doors of the hall. It would have made the house lighter, even more fashionable, to have done so, but its character would have been lost. The heavyweight wood also provides security and stability in bad weather. Where Laurence has made changes, they all relate to the clifftop position of the house. 'All the decoration is devoted to the sea. Blue for the curtains, West Indies blue that you can see down the terrace or through the large pine tree when the weather is beautiful. The sea can be like a light-green or blue lagoon. The water is transparent. We are no longer in the north here but in the south – but what south and where?'

So it could be the Caribbean, the Riviera or one of those sun-filled Greek islands that is being conjured up by the evocative sea blue. To emphasize this illusion the railings of the terrace and its floor are all painted a sharp white, while the décor is nautical: a red-and-white striped tablecloth with a deep fringe is laid with blue glasses to match the sea, a bunch of wild flowers found on the beach and a little model yacht. Behind is a lifebelt with the house's name painted on. For siesta time there are plenty of deck loungers made of teak, their comfortably raked backs and foot-rests cushioned with off-white cotton. And there is an awning to provide shade from the sun on hot days.

Indoors from the terrace is a main living area, where the colours are also brilliant blue and various shades of white. Comfy sofas have soft white covers piped in blue and are set on a diaper-patterned rug in exactly the

same colours. On the white covers are blue cushions and others in the sort of Indian fabric which, 300 years ago, arrived in Marseilles from the East and promptly became Provençal. To these elements add white-painted cabriole-legged French tables, covered with seawashed shells and a collection of cerulean-blue glass, models and paintings of yachts, and white Roman blinds – and you have a room which combines, in one go, sophistication, comfort and the seaside.

The same colours are repeated in the main bedroom – white curtains, a blue diaper wallpaper, blue-and-white bed linen and even a little blue-and-white fabric box, while elsewhere Provençal tablecloths and blue-and-white European and Chinese ceramics are teamed with navigational charts, more seagoing pictures and even blue-and-white carpet bowls.

This is a house given over to holidays and entertaining, always within the rules. 'When the house is *complet*, there must always be half children and animals, half friends.'

The cooking for them is taken seriously. 'The chef and I [like the King and I – but Yves is really king of the house] speak together from the morning to the evening, and after all the meals, to decide on the meal to come next. We analyse the one just finished, point by point: the cooking, the heat of the oven, duration, the aspect of the meat brought to table, its presentation, decoration – and how to

THE ARCHED FIELDS OF THE OAK PANELLING ARE REPEATED BOTH IN THE LARGE DOORS THEMSELVES AND IN THE ARCHES ABOVE THE DOORS OF THE HALL. IT WOULD HAVE MADE THE HOUSE LIGHTER, EVEN MORE FASHIONABLE, TO HAVE PAINTED OVER THEM, BUT ITS CHARACTER WOULD HAVE BEEN LOST.

THIS PAGE AND OPPOSITE
The ground floor of the Breton house is designed and decorated very much in the bourgeois French manner, with heavy panelling and ornate arched doors in the hallway. The panelling in

the dining room is even grander. The Sabourets decided not to paint these in lighter colours but to allow the house to speak for itself. Instead they updated the décor by introducing smart ships' portraits, maritime

maps and models of boats. The family use the house for entertaining – making good use of their Breton blue-and-white pottery, and napkins in the same shades, while even the knives and forks have blue handles.

do better. The *maîtresse de maison* is a Libra, so I always say, "half, half" – balance the diet, share in equal part meat, fish, eggs, *entremets* (sugar or salted) on the week. I want the *feuilletés* of the tart to be as light as the sea air floating on the terrace; when weighed, it is just a feather.

'Red fruit or apricots are bought from Monsieur Collet, who gets fresh vegetables and fruits every day. We frequently have a *potage* for dinner. *Potage Breton aux legumes* is one of our favourites: salted butter in the casserole, vegetables cut into dice. Turn them about for ten minutes then cover them in water – of course, we use the natural mineral water, which comes from a place only 15 km away.'

From the moment the Sabourets wake up in the morning, there is a timetable for the day, even at weekends. 'In the morning, from my bedroom window (we take our breakfast in bed) I chat with the breakfasters on the terrace. The terrace is our "living room" and the meeting point for everybody. The terrace is full south – it's so hot that we wear Breton hats with straw and a velvet ribbon. They read the newspapers that we get at 7.30.'

Next is the question of what everyone will eat – a major French preoccupation. 'I do the shopping list with the cook [her husband, Yves, that is]. I bend from the balcony like a diva in a theatre, with the terrace and the long sandy beach and the musical sound of the water on the rocks, and we argue about the menu.'

THIS PAGE AND OPPOSITE
The colours used throughout the house are virtually restricted to shades of cream and white with brilliant sea blues and turquoises – the shades that inspired Matisse. Very few patterns are allowed to detract from the essential drama of the views from the windows, and the presence of the sea is constantly evoked with groupings of limpet, mussel, scallop and cockle shells, sea-washed pebbles, simple white decoy birds and collections of transparent blue-glass candlesticks, flower vases and lamps.

'All the decoration is devoted to the sea. Blue for the curtains, West Indies blue that you can see through the pine trees when the weather is beautiful. The sea can be like a blue lagoon.'

By 9.30 her daughter, Victoire, has to be at school. 'She says bye-bye on the terrace before going underneath it to take the path to the stairs to the beach. She opens the door to the stairs and my Jack Russell terrier, Big Ben, comes back from his one hour of jogging on the beach between eight and nine. My labrador, Dundee, is already lying on the terrace waiting for me and the eleven o'clock sea bathe.'

Before that, by ten o'clock, says Laurence, the timetable insists that, if the weather is fine, the cushions on the wooden chairs, the beach towels and the parasol – 'Yes, we need one' – are ready for the morning's sunbathing. But it's still not particularly simple. 'I forbid sun oil outside the bathroom (unless they are hidden away in a *trousse*) and I forbid topless – there is the beach for that. I approve of a nice *tenue*.'

Of course. So, as the morning proceeds, Yves and Laurence, their children and guests arrive on the terrace, carefully dressed for a day by the seaside. Although topless is forbidden chez Sabouret, bathing outfits are allowed in the morning.

By lunch, guests and family must have changed again into something a bit less casual. 'At lunchtime, no more bathing suits on the terrace. There should be an adequate conversation – sports, weather, cooking.' A siesta is allowed in the shadows after lunch before *goûter* is made for the children at 4.30. This may consist of '*le célèbre gâteau Breton, les craquelins et les crêpes dentelles*'.

I rather approve of this structured approach to the day. How many times have stays with friends been ruined by meals running hours late and sometimes not even turning up at all? Nothing like that can happen at the Sabourets' house.

After the siesta and *goûter*, there's a pause before guests assemble for yet another meal. Between 7.15 and 7.30 everyone is back on the terrace for cocktails and fruit juices. This will include those who have ignored the siesta in favour of golf, for there is an 18-hole golf course nearby. 'The 16th, 17th and 18th holes are links, made on the sand, and we play along the beach.'

But by 7.30 it's time to admire the view and the position. 'The light at 7.30 is wonderful, pure, gentle for the eyes. The rocks are burning in red and rose, and the air is suspended. The terrace is a boat, diving in the sea, it is the *vigie* which announces the weather. The French flag streams in the wind.'

It could, indeed, come straight from one of those 19th century paintings – a Renoir, perhaps, or a charming corner of an exterior by Vuillard.

OPPOSITE PAGE **One of the few rooms in the house in which pattern has been allowed to take over is the main bedroom, which has a flamboyant, typically French wallpaper. Yet even here the basic blues, creams and whites are in control – to the extent that the shirt hanging in front of the cream-curtained window** **is of exactly the right shade of maritime blue. Here, too, are more model yachts. The floor has been painted simply in white to enhance the strong light from the sea.**

ABOVE **Framed by stately dark-needled pines, the view is, of course, in the same perfect blue and white as the colours of the rooms.**

THE VIEW FROM THE TERRACE IS STUPENDOUS. FRAMED BY THE BRANCHES OF PINES AND THE ROCKY OUTCROPS IS THE SEA BELOW, DOTTED IN SUMMER WITH SCORES OF YACHTS. DURING THE DAY THE SCENE IS ALMOST UNREAL IN ITS BEAUTY – THINK OF AN IDYLLIC FILM SET – WHILE AT NIGHT, ONE BY ONE, THE LIGHTS OF THE BOATS FLICKER ON.

a lighthouse keeper's cottage

A keeper's cottage beside the lighthouse that inspired the artist Edward Hopper has been transformed into a family home without damage to its iconic significance.

Since Pliny the Elder wrote on the subject in the first century AD, living by water for the fun of it has been regarded as the preserve of the rich. Yet the poor live by water too. Their role has been to harvest the seas or to maintain the fishponds, to use waterpower for milling and weaving, to live by fertile coasts when the earth inland is a desert, to look after sea defences and dams – and to guard and protect all those who, from prehistory, have travelled by water and sea. Ferrymen, coastguards, lifeboats and lighthouses are not new. Around 280 BC there was a lighthouse on the island of Pharos,

off Alexandria in Egypt – one of the seven wonders of the world. Lighthouses are always dramatic. They are sited on headlands and at harbour mouths, on dangerous rocks in dangerous seas, and on islands where the tides swirl sandbanks in different directions twice a day. They also mean landfall, a beacon of light in an uncertain world; they offer the hope of safety.

Cape Elizabeth Light is a famous lighthouse – not because it was built by the Lighthouse Stevensons, known for their unwreckable towers and for spawning Robert Louis Stevenson; nor was it like the

OPPOSITE PAGE **A distinctive group of buildings on the rugged coast of Maine, centred on a lighthouse and the lighthouse keeper's home, became very well known when the American artist Edward Hopper painted it in the 20th century. The still-working lighthouse is visible between the main house and a folly.**

THIS PAGE **The current owners have succeeded in adapting the cottage into a family home without destroying its symbolic character. The American flag hangs (or, more often, blows) in front. There are about 4,800 km (3,000 miles) between this lonely light and the next landfall to the east.**

Longstone lighthouse, where, in 1838, the young Englishwoman Grace Darling helped her father rescue shipwrecked sailors from the steamship *Forfarshire*. This lighthouse and the keeper's house at its base were immortalized by the American artist Edward Hopper (1882-1967). According to my *Oxford Companion to Twentieth Century Art*, his work 'has been regarded as a central example of American scene painting, expressing the loneliness, vacuity and stagnation of town life'.

Cape Elizabeth Light does not represent town life, but it certainly is an example of the loneliness that can be found on any American coast or, indeed, on any coast around the world. The remote spots chosen for lighthouses may mean safety for sailors in foundering vessels, but for the lighthouse keeper and his family they represent duty above company, service before society, isolation for an income.

This particular lighthouse stands at the opening of Casco Bay, which lies at the head of Portland Harbour in Maine. It is located in an area of Cape Elizabeth known as 'Two Lights' because in 1874 two lighthouse towers were built about

300 metres (1,000 feet) apart to help sailors to distinguish these lights from those of other nearby lighthouses. Only one remains active, although the other still stands. They are sited to be visible by all shipping in these waters, but, unlike those in the Mediterranean, about 4,800 km (3,000 miles) from the nearest landfall – across the Atlantic Ocean. When the working lighthouse was automated, the small, century-old keeper's cottage that crouches below it against the winds became redundant.

The present owner of the keeper's cottage (but not of the lighthouse itself) came upon it by accident. Or that's how it seemed. 'I grew up in the nearby town,' he says. 'My family lived there for two generations. I was visiting my parents five years ago and decided to go to the ocean to look at the waves – there had been a huge storm. When I drove by the house, which I'd known all my life, I saw a "For Sale" sign. I was just amazed. So I immediately called the broker – and I was lucky enough to purchase the house. It wasn't anything I'd been planning. It wasn't even a decision. I just knew, instinctively, that it was what I wanted.'

THIS PAGE AND OPPOSITE

Waterside houseowners almost always have a pair of binoculars or a telescope trained towards the view. This clifftop house overlooks busy shipping lanes and migratory routes for sea birds. The silhouette of the lighthouse can be seen from many rooms in the house, but, because of its height, the circling beam passes above the roof – so it doesn't keep you awake at night. To add character to the house, the owners have introduced compasses, chronometers and seafarers' instruments.

THIS PAGE AND OPPOSITE
At the centre of the house is a stairwell that is toplit to give light and airiness throughout the building. From here a landing leads into the bedroom of one of the owner's daughters.

Her little rag doll has been tucked up under the coverlet, which has quilted circles reminiscent of sea urchins and shells. Many of the table lamps in the house are adapted from old sea lanterns or hurricane lamps.

Apart from his three daughters, now aged 8, 10 and 12, the owner has numerous relatives in the area, and he wanted to enlarge the house so that it was possible to fit them all in. But, of course, this famous national symbol also had to continue looking as it did in Hopper's painting. So he hired the architectural firm of Stephen Blatt to make the changes.

'Cape Elizabeth Light is one of the most recognizable symbols of Maine's maritime history,' says Blatt. 'Our challenge was to nearly double its size in order to meet his family's needs, take better advantage of the spectacular ocean views and, at the same time, remain sensitive to the historical character of the building. On the interior, we were asked to make the humble lightkeeper's house, which had been insensitively renovated over the years, into one befitting a whaling captain.

'Our solution left the two most public views of the building largely intact. Much of the expansion – including a two-car garage with exercise room above, connecting hall and deck, and screened porch – was placed on the least publicly visible portion of the site. The existing utilitarian basement was also expanded downward and outward to create extra living space on this tight site. The main floor features a dramatic, open-plan two-storey oval rotunda capped by a triangular skylight. The second floor has three children's bedrooms and a master bedroom, all of which open onto the skylit rotunda.

'Interior finishes include antique heart-pine flooring, Douglas fir ceilings and extensive painted woodwork. Careful attention was paid to exterior historical detail – all the trims, including decorative rake-boards, were milled to match the existing profiles.' Blatt took great care to match new stone with the weathered older walls, and the whole was landscaped so that it sat comfortably on its site.

It has been a terrific success for the owner. 'It is very much in keeping with the style and tradition of the old building,' he says. 'It's a truly amazing spot, high up on a hill. The view is as much about the sky, which is incredible, as it is about the ocean. We have a 360-degree view from the high point of the area, a place which just happens to be on the migratory route for birds. We get ducks, geese and wildfowl flying over – any bird which migrates.' The lighthouse itself is, of course, part of this view. 'It's amazingly romantic and charming. In summer, on a clear night, you can sit and watch the light

turning silently and serenely – and, at other times, see it in a raging storm. The light is high enough to shine over the top of the house so the beam doesn't bother us. Then, from that point, you can see three other lights along the coast. Ships are passing all the time, fishing boats, pleasure boats, cruise ships. We are in a position to see the weather systems coming in over the ocean – a low front appears long before it reaches us and you can see thunderheads arriving, too.'

The family appreciates the history of their house: 'There have been only five keepers and their families living here in the hundred years since the house and light were built. We have found their old tools and logbooks from the past. We still have grandchildren of the keepers come to the door and tell us about growing up in the house. This whole area of Maine is rich in maritime history – during the Civil War, 60 per cent of the shipping tonnage was owned by Maine shipowners, and the whole area was a huge and very important trading post.'

Now the house is a second home – but one greatly loved and much used. 'My sister and parents. aunts and uncles all live around here. We're up here all the time with our children. At Thanksgiving, for example, we had a dinner party for 25. We do any kind of activity you can think of – cross-country and downhill skiing, boating, hiking and camping.'

Originally, Stephen Blatt says, the whole idea of extending and changing this famous house was highly controversial with the preservationists. 'The end product is a testament to the notion that historic buildings can successfully evolve with changing times and lifestyles.' If they don't, I would add, there's no hope for them but an existence as a sterile museum. But here the combination of architect and owner has created a living family home which not only gives pleasure to the present generation but also secures a viable future for Cape Elizabeth Light and the keeper's cottage for their second century.

THIS PAGE AND OPPOSITE
The main bedroom has panoramic views over the clifftops to the busy sea lanes below. Everything – walls, woodwork and beamed ceilings – is painted white to enhance the effect of the waves and ripples of water below. Here, as elsewhere, the colours are kept to a single strong blue, with the only pattern being a bed cover of mixed shells. Given the strong character of the exterior, the owners have collected lots of little lighthouses and Hopper artefacts such as books and stamps. as well as green glass objects to recall seawashed bottles.

'It's amazingly romantic and charming. In summer, on a clear night, you can sit and watch the light turning silently and serenely - and, at other times, see it in a raging storm.'

Europeans have been enchanted by the Caribbean ever since they first discovered it in the 15th century. In the case of Barbados, the island nearest to Europe, it was the Portuguese who arrived first – they called it 'Los Barbados' (The Bearded Ones) after the large groves of bearded fig trees which grew there. In 1605, however, the English arrived on the island, and held it as a colony from 1628 until independence in 1966.

It is one of the most beautiful and friendly of all the West Indian islands: not threatening like the volcanic island of Martinique, where Mont Pelée erupted in 1902 and killed 20,000 of its people, nor violent, as Jamaica has become. It is soft and low – the highest point is only 436 metres (1,430 feet) above sea level – and yet fertile from the volcanic dust shed by nearby St Vincent which has settled on its coral limestone. The coral reefs that virtually encircle the whole island protect it from the worst of the storms, yet the north-east trade winds temper the tropical heat from winter to mid spring.

The houses in this book have been divided into categories dependent on their positions – because living on a river is an entirely different experience from living by a lake. You might also think that living on a cliff made it impossible to be beside a beach. But this house in Barbados has managed to find the best of both situations – a clifftop site which has incredible views and colours both day and night, along with direct access to a beach in an island where the beaches are the most romantic in the world. Think

palms, coral and calypso

A luxurious villa stands high above a broad expanse of soft white sand bordered on one side by a brilliant sea and on the other by a garden ablaze with tropical colour.

OPPOSITE PAGE **The 'Georgian' cantilevered staircase leads from a hall with a coral-stone floor to the upstairs bedrooms. A specially commissioned Barbadian table (decorated with gardenia flowers) is placed at exactly the correct focal point. Terraces, pools, pots of plants are all there to frame the view.**

THIS PAGE **Houses in Barbados are specially designed to take advantage of every breath of breeze to cool the interiors. This new home – built in the vernacular style – has a heavy pediment to the open porch which is intended to reduce the effects of sunlight. Large airy rooms extend beyond it.**

'The architecture reflects everything that is typically Barbadian
- coral floors, plaster walls, trellis and balustrade balconies,
with a lunch gazebo and beautifully landscaped tropical gardens.'

of soft white sand bordered on one side by a brilliant, unpolluted sea and on the other by tropical foliage at its most colourful. Add a few palms whispering in the breeze as they grow from the sand, and a distant hint of calypso, and you get, enviously, the idea of the position of Gardenia.

It was the sheer brilliance of the site that attracted the present owners and their children to the untouched land at St James on the island. 'It had the advantage of reasonable width and a good depth, which meant that there was a fair distance between the noise of the road and the sea,' they explain. 'The site is on two levels, with the house built far enough from the road on the top of a small cliff – about 18 metres (60 feet) from sea level. Some of the services like car parking and the tennis court are kept well away from the house, but from the front door we can step straight out and down into our garden.'

One level of the garden is on a terrace below the house; the owners can push through a small gate and walk right down to the beach and the sea beyond. Also, because the house is high and the garden and beach are below eye-level, they can fling open the front doors of the house and the view is of the brilliant tropical seas all around.

'People say that no one has ever quite achieved their dream home – but we have. On a nice day the water is a beautiful blue. Near the front are coral reefs which break the seas in rough weather and give us some protection, while in normal weather, there's always an interesting ripple over the coral with soft breakers rolling towards us.' Even though the couple have the most enticing swimming pool, they, family and friends are always swimming and snorkelling in the water beyond the beach because it is so safe.

The house has deliberately been built in old Barbadian style. 'The architect wanted to protect the West Indies style and materials, and we tried to do that.' The architect was Larry Warren (two other houses in Barbados designed by him are shown on pages 154–59 and 178–85). He, too, was enraptured by the 'fantastic' site. 'The view towards the beach and sea is panoramic and yet close – you actually hear the waves lapping on the coral reefs at low tide. The experience at sunset is unimaginable.'

He designed the building to take advantage of these delights. The main living and dining rooms, generous verandahs and the bedrooms all open onto the view and gardens. 'The architecture reflects everything that is Barbadian – coral floors, plaster walls, trellis and balustrade balconies with a lunch gazebo and lovely gardens, compliments of Fernando Tabora, the well-known South American landscaper, who created a tropical experience of space, colour, texture and shape in the gardens .'

Thanks to the design of the garden, the area teems with wildlife. 'The birds are superb,' says one of the owners. 'There are plenty of hummingbirds, and even the odd monkey in the garden. We have palms, bougainvillea and flame trees all around us.'

THIS PAGE AND OPPOSITE
Growing exotic plants is no problem in the tropics – the problem is to stop them growing. Here leafy palms in pots and in the garden itself help to shade a handy bar beside the pool. The constant heat of the day is counteracted by planting masses of shady foliage – and, of course, providing a good supply of rum laced with tropical fruit juices (or, if you must, fruit juices not laced with rum).

The couple were also keen that the interior design of the house was firmly in the West Indian tradition. They even had locally designed furniture made by the island firm of Dawn and Ed Pionkowski. The result is a whole series of breezy and light rooms to give solace in the heat – all of them inspired by the various architectural influences that have affected the West Indies.

Colonial French and British 18th-century designs with flamboyant chandeliers and ceramics combine with the lush and exotic greenery which taps on the windows and finds its way indoors in the shape of house plants. The whole has been designed to maximize the sense of relaxation and ease amid the tropical heat – a feature found in the best Caribbean design.

Another major attraction for the owners is the golf courses spread around Barbados. 'The main one we go to is the Royal Westmorland, one of three world-class courses on the island, and another is planned at Sandy Lane. There are also two smaller ones.'

Barbados is a perfect retreat for Britons and Americans because there is so much that is familiar, while the setting and the weather are luxuriantly tropical. Everyone speaks English, as they have since the 17th century. Local architecture and design are heavily influenced by Georgian styles and are also reminiscent of the plantation houses of America's Deep South. In this house there are arches with glazed fanlights similar to those in Edinburgh townhouses and to the *oeil-de-boeuf* oval windows that appear above porticoes in Britain's stately homes. Floors are tiled in patterns adapted in the 18th century from Moorish originals, and grand chandeliers hanging from the centres of ceilings do not look at all out of place.

The owners and their family and friends have come to love the island and its people. 'It's a relaxing country, and the people are extremely pleasant and considerate with an easy-going style. As well as the golf, there are world-class restaurants and lovely beaches.'

THIS PAGE **The guest bedroom has a light, airy décor, a stone floor, and louvred French windows. Heavily fringed palms and other exotic plants are the work of the garden designer Fernando Tabora.**

OPPOSITE PAGE **Houses in the tropics are built with heavy overhanging verandahs which allow all windows and doors to be left open without the need of breeze-inhibiting blinds. Guests in this house are heavily pampered. This shady open area has been designed especially for their relaxation and includes everything from lounging chairs to lanterns for evening star-spotting.**

beachside living

Living by a beach is like being on holiday all year round. In the early morning you can get up at dawn and walk along sands wet with the tide and busy with wading birds pecking for food; at midday you can watch the world go by from the vantage of your own verandah, as you drink white wine and eat olives untouched by blown sand. And, at night, left alone once more, you can watch the sun go down and the moon glinting on the waves. 'If only,' those of us condemned to cities will cry.

Elena Colombo, imprisoned in New York during working hours, found the perfect retreat in an old industrial site close to – but utterly different from – the ultra-chic Hamptons. Here, among friends, she messes about in what her father calls 'that shack', recycling furniture from thrift stores and combing the beach for wave-washed glass and sea-bleached wood.

It's pretty much the same for Philip Hooper, who discovered a unique house on England's south coast, designed in 1958 to combine elements of house and ship. The whole is filled with brilliant light from windows in all four walls, but the main wall at the front, which faces the beach, is glass from floor to ceiling. The garden, on the other hand, is pure 2001, an exotic mixture of spikes and swords among driftwood, sand and gravel.

David Davies lives beside the water both in London and in his country home on the Sussex coast. His house looks directly out over the sloping pebbles that make up the beach in this area, heavy groynes saving the land from the ravages of the sea. Inside, the cool white space is enlivened with reminders of the sea: driftwood and tiny model ships, shells and pebbles. A formal garden breaks the contact between house and beach, with box bushes and brick paths leading the eye towards the horizon.

Leave the sometimes bleak English seaside behind and holiday in tropical Barbados – as did the owners of Four Winds. Here, from shaded verandahs, as they wait for the sun sink in the west, they watch the waves breaking over the coral reefs and the hummingbirds drinking the nectar of flowers. Their home is a reminder of the style Europe gave to the West Indies – and how the easy living altered the architecture to suit the island life.

Waverley, a group of three houses melded into holiday cottages which lead directly to a soft-sanded beach, is also in Barbados. This residence was designed by the Bajan architect Larry Warren, whose own home was adapted from another historic house on the island. He is determined to conserve and adapt the old designs before they disappear entirely.

life's a Long Island beach

For busy, harassed city-dwellers, nothing could be more therapeutic than to escape to this secluded corner of New England, where the beach remains the focal point of community life throughout the long days of summer.

THIS PAGE AND OPPOSITE Her father calls Elena Colombo's house, part of a Long Island community, 'that shack'. Well, it is a shack – but in the nicest possible way. It has survived the seas for a century and suits the locals' friendly lifestyle.

The houses here were originally built as homes for workers at a nearby brick factory, and the new owners work hard to keep them simple. Being part of a fixed group of friends, however, means there is lots of easy entertaining, too.

Something about living beside water attracts opposite extremes. At one end of the spectrum is the person who loves solitude and contemplation and is inclined to a certain reclusiveness – why go anywhere else if you have tranquillity and beauty all around? At the other end are those who desire to share their luck with family and friends. To some extent the attitude varies according to the kind of waterside place that's chosen. It's easier to be alone on a clifftop or beside a still lake than it is to be alone by a beach. Ever since the Victorians took the plunge in their bathing machines, beaches have been about holidays, fun, children, expeditions and parties.

There could not be a better example of the beach as the focal point in the life of a community than Elena Colombo's chosen place on the shores of eastern Long Island, only two hours' drive from the centre of New York. It is one of 31 old cottages that make up an entire community. This is not a community that consists simply of an informal group of people and houses like, say, a village or a block of flats; this is a legally grouped commune that owns common land and has a ruling board voted in to make decisions.

The cottages were built about 100 years ago to house workers in a brick factory. By all accounts the workers didn't stay very long – perhaps because, in winter, this can be a fierce place where neither warmth nor running water can survive the frozen pipes. So when the family that ran the brick business realized that it could not keep workers in its tied cottages, it began to find holiday tenants, drawn to the area by the proximity of the burgeoning city of

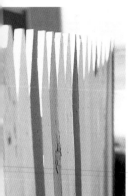

New York. 'It became a recreational summer home very soon after it was built,' says Elena Colombo. 'The brick works has gone – it's now a marina – but bricks are still washed up all over the beaches and the shore. We gather them to make patios and walkways – so, in theory, the brick works are still with us.'

The cluster of cottages continued to be owned by the original family until a few years ago. 'Two New York developers came and spoke to the owners and made them a bid. They then told us tenants that they were thinking of selling – and we panicked. We organized ourselves into a motley crew and found a way of making a down payment and buying the property. The owners kept five cottages. Some tenants had to leave, but most of us managed to buy our homes. It was a very disruptive period for all of us.'

The present position is that most people who live here own their houses – some of which are rented out to holidaymakers – but 36 hectares (90 acres) of land around the houses are communally owned, each owner having the equivalent of a shareholding in the total. All the community members can therefore walk wherever they please, other than in the small garden plots beside the houses.

'I am currently on the board – in charge of road maintenance,' says Elena, a sculptor, with an amazed chuckle. The board is responsible for keeping up the infrastructure, such as roads and walkways, and for deciding who will buy cottages as they come up for sale. 'We have a list of people who want to buy houses. People who buy have to be agreed, voted in by all of us.' This is less alarming than it might seem for, says Elena, the community is 'very, very casual – run like a cooperative. We all meet each other, have no restrictions, and people understand that. That's why we're such a diverse group.' The character of the community – verging on a hippy commune, she adds – is so definite that 'people either get it

THIS PAGE AND OPPOSITE **One of Elena Colombo's enthusiasms is picking up various attractive items of junk that can be used to decorate the house. Locals swap their furniture and bits and pieces by taking them down to a community centre where everything is up for grabs, while the nearby thrift** shops are heavily patronized by members of the community. The original kitchen sink (above) is enlivened with daffodil-yellow walls and propped pictures, while the main kitchen area (opposite) doubles as a dining room with plain wooden chairs and an old round mirror above a high stool.

'I can hardly begin to expound on the positives of living by the water. The smell, the colours, the opportunity to sit and watch the birds, the sailboats, the fresh fish, the sun, the breeze.'

or they don't'. Those who don't 'get it' probably don't want to join in anyway. Elena comments that her father is one of the latter, calling her beloved cottage 'that shack'.

This is purely a summer community, for the cottages are not 'winterized': there is insufficient insulation to keep rooms warm in winter, and the plastic water pipes are still inclined to freeze up, which means no running water. People do venture out in the cold, but usually to rough it for a hot picnic in front of a warm fire or for a single night snuggled in goosedown.

So only in summer does the place come fully alive, which is why it has such a carefree holiday atmosphere. The cottages are various sizes. Three of them are very large, each with a floor area of about 110 square metres (1,200 square feet), while the rest have only one or two rooms and total floor areas of about 28 square metres

(300 square feet). Most are decorated, just like Elena Colombo's, with casual finds from the beach and the water, and from the small local stores. I get the impression that, rather than trying to outdo each other in acquiring special objects, members of this community compete to find the least expensive décor. 'My place isn't at all fancy. The decorations come from the thrift stores that benefit local charities such as the animal shelter. I am a sculptor, and I'm starting to dot my property with pieces inspired by the wind and water. I use metal, stone, wood and bone found on or near the property.

'Everybody does the same because a single shell on a shelf looks beautiful here. The houses are so simple, so old, with 12-pane windows and wainscoting put in at the turn of the century, that simple decoration suits them. People here regularly go to the dump [formally known as the town recycling centre] and the local antique shop for finds – and there's The Barn, where people take things they no longer want. Others will go to pick things up, so everything circulates. We're into the whole recycling vibe. There are yard sales, too, where everything is real cheap – 5 cents – and bartering is big. It's very catch-as-catch-can, and nobody wants to be elegant.'

Even Elena's dog was discovered on the shore. 'My old dog Lucky, who died here this summer, I adopted seven years ago (he was already living on the shore here) and he was loved by all.

OPPOSITE PAGE **Elena Colombo prides herself on using found objects to decorate the house. Some are picked up on the beach, others come from local thrift stores. The back porch shows the powerful effect that can be achieved by the artful arrangement of simple objects such as old candlesticks and tools.**

THIS PAGE **In the front porch a wire salad shaker doubles as a wall sculpture and an oil lamp stands on a white table; flowery cushions are piled on a cheerful striped blanket. Details of *objets trouvés* in the back porch include a polite notice, a window with a star silhouetted against the light and a bucketful of shells.**

I sprinkled him over the property so he will be there for ever. Everyone in the community came and paid their respects to him with pats, bones, bacon and love.

'What makes living by the water particularly special for me is the people I live next to and the reverence we have for our slice of paradise – not to mention the fact that when I open my eyes in the morning all I see is an uninterrupted view of the water.'

Many of the owners are artists. 'There are a lot of photographers and people in the film industry, painters, a woman who is on to her second screenplay, and a writer of children's books. There are decorators and designers, a psychiatrist and an acupuncturist, a massage therapist and antique dealers.' Elena thinks that if all the owners put out signs advertising what they could do, you'd have access to every skill you might ever need.

'Many of us are friends from Manhattan, and we have gotten to know everyone and live side by side. We have beautiful sparkly dinners out on the lawns, when we all bring something to eat and set up long tables. There are kids and old people, gays and straights, blacks and whites, and everything in between. The oldest person is 85, and often the youngest has just been born. It is a true commune.

'There are spontaneous parties all the time, when everybody goes to everybody else's place. One friend always brings fireworks, and another has a huge grill – so we go to the local fish store and just throw the fish on the grill. It's possible to fish in our inlet. At 5.30 am you'll see the boats chugging in the water out front. There's flounder and bluefish to be had and, in the bay, bass and blowfish – what we call chicken of the sea. There are mussels and clams and lobster out near the sound.' Also around the shores you can find porgies and red snapper, swordfish and tuna and the tantalizingly named weakfish. Diamond-back sea turtles are in the sea here, too.

Much of the land is still farmed, and there are vineyards everywhere. 'There are miles and miles of grapes, and the vegetables grown around here probably supply the whole of the rest of Long Island.' Elena Colombo has her own small garden where she grows tomatoes, peppers, peas and beans with squashes in autumn. 'Everyone has a herb bed – the plants seem to love it out here, perhaps it's the salty air.' And herbs are swapped around between the community, too. 'I grew ten tomatoes this year – not a lot – but it was terrific to walk out and pluck one to make a salad and eat it on my own kitchen table.

'I can hardly begin to expound on the positives of living by the water. The smell, the colours, the opportunity to sit and watch the birds, the sailboats, the fresh fish, the sun, the breeze.' Quite a few of the commune people are keen birdwatchers, and on my behalf Elena asked them (the commune at work again) what species were about the place. These included sea eagles, also known as ospreys,

OPPOSITE PAGE **A guest** bedroom has been decorated with sea-green beaded walls, and, to reinforce the air of informality, an old mirror has been propped between the beds. Although many articles have been retrieved from skips, the fan quilt was an exceptional buy.

THIS PAGE **Original** tongue-and-groove walls have been painted a soft white, as has the plain iron bedstead in Elena's bedroom. Elena has used her clever eye to add a simple table with an old-fashioned lamp to a single picture, an impressive straw hat and a wicker chair.

GOOD-NIGHT

THIS PAGE **Like a giant galvanized bucket, the bathtub fits neatly into the tiny bathroom, which is festooned with bright beach towels and primitive pictures. When the weather is good, Elena prefers to take a shower outside.**

OPPOSITE PAGE **Many of the rooms in the house retain original features, such as wooden planks and built-in cupboards. The charm comes from Elena's clever use of painted walls and furniture.**

snow egrets and the great blue heron; there are belted kingfishers, loons and willow flycatchers, too.

'There are a couple of boats out here owned by friends that we can all pile into and zip to another spot across the water to swim or picnic. Two are beautiful restored mahogany runabouts that match the property out here.'

Indeed, the whole community could not be less like the frenetic and famous Hamptons, which are close in distance but light years away in terms of atmosphere. 'New York has been obsessed with the Hamptons' glitz and glamour for so many years that no one paid any attention to the rest of the area. It just plodded on alone, all by itself – even though it's warmer and sunnier here, no one can figure out why.' The Hamptons are now

expensive, smart and overdeveloped; their loss has been this small community's gain. Elena Colombo is lyrical about it all. 'The light out here takes my breath away. The weather can change in an instant. We have everything from still, hot, humid days to driving hail and hurricanes. The cottages have weathered many storms, and sometimes it feels as if they are protected by a higher power, or maybe they were just built right.'

What is so special here is the feeling not just of friendship but of shared responsibility and the enjoyment that comes from being part of a close-knit group. This is like a family, but one whose members are chosen for their likemindedness. While they love the joint meals around the shore and the pleasures of meeting

friends on holiday, they are also very concerned about the environment. Hence everyone swaps household furniture and necessities, trawls the seashore for found objects, shells, driftwood and old fishing gear, and patronizes the charities' thrift stores.

Elena was extremely concerned to ensure that I didn't reveal the exact location of this little bit of paradise – everyone's privacy must be preserved, she said. I reckon that, if the owners of those 31 cottages have been clever enough to find a small part of the world where the pressures are minimal and the pleasures great, there is no good reason why I should disturb that.

'Whenever I come here, I just don't want to leave. I feel so lucky,' Elena concludes. Lucky, certainly – but luck has to be looked for.

a haven cooled by trade winds

Built of coral limestone, the house incorporates some of
the classic elements of the plantation houses – verandahs,
shutters, shingled roofs and a courtyard colonnade.

THIS PAGE AND OPPOSITE **The building that Four Winds replaced was the
very first hotel on the island of Barbados, but it had fallen into a state of such
serious decay that, despite local opposition, it had to be demolished and
recreated. The Barbadian architect Larry Warren is in such good touch with**
the island's architecture that the new building not only won him a heritage award
but also gained the approval of local people. The heavy portico of the main door,
which is overscaled to reduce the effects of the sun, is actually inward-looking –
forming one side of a courtyard – rather than turned out towards the ocean.

The Caribbean island of Barbados has developed its own traditional style of architecture that relies heavily on local materials. The most important building material is coral limestone, which is textured and porous – and this was the material used for an old house on Gibbs Beach, St Peter, considered by those who know to be one of the most beautiful and favoured beaches on the entire island.

To the dismay of architect Larry Warren – whose mission is to conserve and retain the vernacular Barbadian architecture – the old house, built as the island's first hotel, was past saving. 'The original house was an early-20th-century coral-stone building which was damaged by the subsequent owners to such an extent that it had to be demolished.'

The local people were not at all happy that it should be taken down, and there was fierce opposition. 'From the outset the demolition of the historic residence provoked a lot of criticism, so I took up the challenge to try to replace it – hopefully, with a residence that could quickly grow into the role.'

One advantage of the demolition was that the new owners could buy further properties next to the ruined house, giving the architect the chance to increase the size of the new building. 'This allowed me to maximize the views at the Headland to the Caribbean Sea, provide spacious gardens and other facilities such as The Cottage and a tennis court.'

An expert on Barbadian architecture, Warren was able to create a new house that has actually enhanced the island's heritage. 'I based the architecture on the Barbadian style, with verandahs, shutters, shingled roofs – classic elements found in some of the plantation houses. The courtyard colonnade and the staircase are representative of this.' Warren found that the secret was to create a 'history' for the house in his own imagination in order to develop its character. 'I played with the "story" of how the open courtyard was from an "earlier" period and subsequently enclosed. The telltales are the gutters, which drain internally, creating a pleasant sound of water during a rainstorm and, externally, the coral-stone "eyebrows", which show evidence of some departure from the rest of the house.'

This courtyard is a fine and generous space where a central staircase with light-green trelliswork banisters reminiscent of 18th-century northern European design – a combination, perhaps, of French, English and Swedish influences – doglegs upwards. All around the courtyard are classical columns, made of near-white coral stone, which create spacious corridors, tiled with more coral stone.

The whole effect of the courtyard is to create an exotic, tropical version of the grand hall of an English Georgian country house. Other similar columns are used to hold up the shady verandahs around the

house which allow the owners to take advantage of the cooling trade winds and shade while looking out over the beach. The green latticework also turns up on other, less stately verandahs.

'The house lives up to its name, Four Winds,' says one of the owners. 'There's always a nice breeze.' She finds it an incredibly relaxing place to be, a place to overwinter when Britain is at is most dreary. 'It's nice to hear the waves at night, very soothing. I always sleep like a log when I'm here. The beach is one of the prettiest on the whole island, with tropical palms and white sand. It's also quiet because we don't get many visitors.'

What they do get is plenty of animals, wild and domestic. 'We have two macaws in an aviary, which we let out to fly quite often, even if it is a bit dangerous. They may decide not to come back. Then there are tortoises in the garden. We have a breeding pair which are about two feet long and they have had lots of little ones. There are plenty of hummingbirds too.

'Sadly, there are no pelicans any more, even though they are the national birds of Barbados. They used to nest on a sandspit, but since it was incorporated in the port they have left the island and moved on. At certain times of the year there are whales and sometimes flying fish which, from the boat, we can see skimming over the water. We also catch tuna and dorado (they're called dolphin fish, but they aren't dolphins) to eat.'

The site had been occupied for a hundred years, so there were fine, mature trees all around the area. 'There are palms and manicheels, sea almonds and big shady mahogany trees. Some of then grow straight out of the sand of the beach. It's so lovely that we swim in the sea all the time and hardly ever use the pool.'

The tropics are even more romantic by night, when the air grows cooler and less humid, and the glare of the sun gives way to bright moonlight and brilliant stars. 'We look out west towards the sunsets and wait for that wonderful moment – a green flash – when the sun goes down. I saw that just two nights ago.'

The owners were clever in commissioning the interior decorator Chester Jones, the biographer of the design firm of Colefax and Fowler, who has been heavily influenced by their eclectic style. Since John Fowler was the pioneer of the typical English country-house décor which that firm successfully exported all over the world, the

OPPOSITE PAGE The living room has French windows on three sides – all with arched 'Georgian' fanlights over them – and faces out over the ocean. This design ensures that breezes are encouraged, keeping the room relatively cool.

THIS PAGE The dining room is reached from the living room and has its walls trellised for effect. A large arched doorway keeps the whole area light and airy, while candles are used to give soft lighting at night. The owners have used all sorts of local shell, fossil and seaside motifs in lamps, coasters and pictures.

COLOUR SCHEMES ARE DELICIOUSLY COOL, BUT THE EXOTIC LOCATION IS ALLUDED TO IN A SUDDEN BRIGHT SPLASH OF COLOUR – SCARLET, LIME, OCHRE AMONG THE CUSHIONS AND CHAIRS, WHILE FLAMBOYANT FLAME-TREE BLOSSOMS FILL THE VASES.

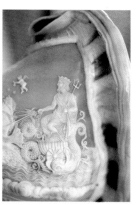

choice could not have been better. Jones has taken the basics of English country and adapted them to the West Indies. Where a British dining room often has – ironically – mahogany dining chairs and table, this house has a far lighter, fresher wood table and wicker chairs that are cooler to sit in. Wicker is also used for lounging chairs and daybeds on the verandahs.

The colour schemes are deliciously cool: striped Mediterrean-blue rugs on the floor, blue-and-white gingham and natural calico covering the chairs and sofas. But the exotic location is alluded to in a sudden bright splash of colour – scarlet, lime, ochre among the cushions and chairs, while flame-tree blossoms fill the vases.

The huge and intricate shells of the tropics are also brought into the house, as once the Georgians created shell bath-houses and grottoes. They form the decoration for mirrors and console tables, and fill up white-painted cupboards in the manner of 17th-century cabinets of curiosities. Here there are giant conches and clams, branches of local coral and the beautiful striped shells of the nautilus. Shells also make their appearance on glasses and bowls.

The family remove from England to their tropical hideaway each year from Christmas until Easter. Mother and father, four children, three of whom are married, and five grandchildren – are all expected for Christmas, when 20 will sit down to a traditional dinner of turkey, but eaten in the evening when the thermometer has gone down. 'It's a happy holiday home for us,' the owner says. 'We have a wonderful staff who look after us, and we're surrounded by cheerful people.'

The last word must go to Larry Warren, whose faith in his vernacular building has confounded all the local jeremiahs who complained so vehemently. 'The residence was on the National Trust Open House Programme, so I hope that has gone some way towards tempering the initial criticism.' Four Winds is a superb example of a late-20th-century Barbadian house that has learned so much from the past.

THIS PAGE Bathrooms are
very important in the tropics
and this huge main one has a
central bath with an *oeil de
boeuf* window above it. The
bath is placed in such a way
that it allows the owners
to look out through French
windows and see the waves
of the sea beyond. The
beautiful floor is mosaic.

OPPOSITE PAGE Local coral
stone was used to make
pillars in the hall, while
shells have been grafted
onto mirror frames, as was
common in the 18th century.

an English bucolic idyll

If you ask people who live beside water what the attractions are, they are often moved to lyricism – this way of life is undoubtedly addictive.

Philip Hooper is a man who, I would guess, does not wax lyrical all that easily. But here he is talking about Beach House, perched above a shingle beach outside Hastings, on the south coast of England: the place where William the Conqueror landed in 1066, and near where the last English king, Harold, lost his final battle and his life – a place resonant with history.

'It's a constantly changing panorama. The sea is always different. Just now it's a milky turquoise, and the sky is just turning pink with dusk. There are clouds on the horizon, but above us the sky is still pale blue.

'Boats are constantly moving up and down because this coast is a major shipping route. We get container vessels and liners sailing past on the horizon. Lots of activity. This is also a light-aircraft

THIS PAGE **Beach House is a modern house in a historic setting, close to where, in 1066, William of Normandy defeated King Harold of England. The house makes full use of its dramatic position, with full-frontal views from every storey.**

OPPOSITE PAGE **An old car port has been converted to make a cobbled outdoor dining area; prying eyes are diverted by the exotic and abundant garden.**

'The Downs and the Weald and the marshes are all within a small area. Freshwater pools on Romney Marsh are stopovers for migrating birds. On the beach are oystercatchers, dunlins and wading birds.'

route, so we have planes flying above us. The beach has lots of activity too: people going along by the sea wall, promenading, windsurfing, kites, people walking their dogs. We can sit back and watch it all.'

Philip and his partner, Alan Fergusson, have made their house into a comfortable observatory the better to see – but not necessarily to take part in – all this activity. Its main living room, which takes up the entire third floor of the house, has glass windows all around, beyond which is an open balcony. A sensible black solid-fuel iron stove is placed in the perfect position for people to sit beside while beach-watching in the winter and during the violent storms that lash this coast from time to time.

The house itself is almost certainly unique. It was designed in 1958 by Michael Patrick, an architect who was more a theoretician and teacher than a hands-on designer. Indeed, the family who commissioned him to create this house (and who sold it to Hooper, an interior designer, six years ago) believe that Patrick never built another house.

It is also curious in the context of the time at which it was built. In 1958 Britain was still recovering from the Second World War, and the austerity programmes inflicted on the country by politicians. Most homes built during this period were strictly practical – which this house is not. 'It is more reminiscent of American houses than British ones,' says Hooper.

Its entire purpose is to take advantage of its stunning position. Unconventionally, the living room is at the very top of the house because this is where the best views are. Each wall is made of glass, although only in the sea-facing wall does the glazing reach from floor to ceiling. The other three walls have chest-high tongue-and-groove wooden dados with windows above. In typical 1950s style, the windows are shallow and wide. Hooper has fitted all of them with dark-pink Venetian blinds, also very 1950s, and painted the

THIS PAGE AND OPPOSITE
Since the film-maker Derek Jarman created his shingle garden overlooking a nearby shore in the 1980s, beachside gardening has undergone a revolution. This seaside garden incorporates many of Jarman's motifs, including sea-washed pebbles, cork floats, flotsam and jetsam.

However, Philip Hooper has unified the whole by using a background colour of pale turquoise with added dashes of brilliant cobalt such as in this Moroccan bowl. The greyer shade of blue in the spiky agave plant, and the lilac-tinged scallop shells, complement the colours of the seashore beyond.

window frames a sea blue. 'One of my clients – a graphic designer – taught me a trick about windows. He said that, if a window frame is painted a dark colour, then the landscape beyond becomes more important and the frame itself less dominant. Originally this large light space was all white, but I felt the need to darken it, which made it less shed-like and more solid, less aware of its shape.'

Hooper also moved the main kitchen, mostly used as a utility room, down to the ground floor, leaving only a serving kitchen – with fridge, hotplate, sink – in the room alongside the dining area.

He has, however, kept all the 1950s room dividers, often with cupboards and sliding doors, and the unmistakable period character has been enhanced by the period furniture and decorations.

'I had two houses before, one in London and the other in Devon, which were Arts and Crafts in period, late Victorian. When I found this house I sold everything I had collected of that period at auction and started again. The house is so strong that, to work, it needed strong things in it. I was ripe to change direction and, I think, I have a history of getting to styles first, before the public does. I seek out things that others aren't aware of.' The furniture in the living room includes two Robin Day chairs, once upholstered in orange but now a soft donkey brown, and a daybed by Capellini.

Everywhere there are pieces of 1950s pottery and brilliantly coloured Venetian glass. Many of the vases, bowls and lights are also by Italian and French designers. 'When I started collecting the 1950s, I thought English pieces were a bit bleak, so I went for French and Italian, which are more sexy.'

Below this eyrie, the first floor holds all the bedrooms and bathrooms. Originally there were four bedrooms, but one has become a dressing room. The bedrooms, all small, have been left as they

THIS PAGE AND OPPOSITE **Philip Hooper's house is a virtuoso display by** an architect who appears never to have designed another domestic building. Since it was commissioned by the previous owners, virtually nothing has been changed. Hooper has been astute enough to refer back to the 1950s with his spiky cactuses and windows shaded by Venetian blinds. Most of the fittings are original, and Hooper has emphasized their character by the use of quirky art pottery of the period. Like other waterside homeowners, he has been strongly influenced by the style of the house.

'One of my clients, a graphic designer, taught me a trick about windows: if a window frame is painted a dark colour, the landscape beyond becomes more important and the frame itself less dominant.'

were designed by Michael Patrick, who was clearly inspired by the interiors of ships and smaller yachts. The whole house uses tongue-and-groove wood on the walls, but the bedrooms have built-in bunks raised high above useful storage areas, and once again the windows provide splendid views. Venetian blinds take the place of curtains here also.

Philip Hooper's house has far more than sea views. 'The back of the house faces onto the South Downs and their grazing sheep. It's very bucolic. I wanted it for its 360-degree views as well as its proximity to the sea. We have the landscape of the Downs and the Weald, along with marshes, all in a small area. There are freshwater pools on Romney Marsh that are stopovers for migrating birds. On the beach there are oystercatchers, dunlins and wading birds.'

The ground floor is the least exciting part of the house, but an old carport has been transformed into an outside dining area complete with nautical allusions, and the original cobbled floor remains below the table. Beyond it stretches an extraordinarily exotic garden – more Havana than Hastings – which, says Alan Fergusson, was designed partly to distract passers-by from peering into the 'goldfish bowl' of the house. Though it seems larger, it is only 20 metres (66 feet) long and 17 metres (55 feet) wide, but Hooper's design both blocks the view and leads the eye onwards to the beach.

Running beside the outside dining area is a straight canal filled with colourful Koi carp. The sweeps of shingle beyond it are planted with the sort of spiky-leaved plants that can cope with such sharp

THIS PAGE AND OPPOSITE
In keeping with the style of the 1950s – the period when this beachside house was built – virtually every wall has its wide, shallow windows. These vary from full-length ones, which provide expansive views of the beaches of England's south coast, to chest-high ones that look away from the sea, focusing attention inland, on the fields and hills beyond the garden. Philip Hooper is an avid collector of Contemporary pottery from the 1950s, including works from Poole and Rye potteries, along with Venetian glass and period furniture.

THE BEDROOMS, ALL SMALL, HAVE BEEN LEFT AS THEY WERE
DESIGNED BY MICHAEL PATRICK, WHO WAS CLEARLY INSPIRED
BY THE INTERIORS OF SHIPS AND SMALLER YACHTS.

drainage; there are yuccas and cordylines underplanted with grey santolina and eschscholzia. Everywhere driftwood, standing upright, leads the eye towards the beach. These pieces have been dragged from the shingle beyond and decorated with shells and stones, which Hooper has brought back from travels all over the world – most recently Antigua. He also collects stones with holes running through them – fairy stones that are believed to bring luck. These are threaded onto clipped hawthorn bushes and appear only when the leaves are shed in autumn.

Many of the other plants are evergreen, with strongly shaped leaves and strong growth patterns, while other grey Mediterranean groupings are kept from flowering by disciplined clipping. The whole is sheltered by evergreen holm oaks and Scots pines along with tamarisk and *Euonymous japonicus*, which can survive sea winds.

In true beach mode, walls and furniture (some designed by Philip) are painted in bright blues and yellows. The garden designer John Brookes praises the garden for its 'essence of place'. It 'encompasses not only what will grow best in a given place without improvement but what, in terms of hard as well as soft materials, looks right there too. So, from the juxtaposition of its plants, overlaying a strong and simple design in a complex location, the owners have created something of real and lasting charm.' It looks as good in February – from the shelter of the living room perched three floors above and warmed by its open-doored stove – as it does in high summer for picnics. And the spiky indoor cactus brings the same exoticism indoors for winter.

Philip Hooper does have a London *pied-à-terre*, but it's not a boring bedsit or a flat in a mansion block. When he must stay in the city, his chosen base is a narrowboat.

OPPOSITE PAGE **The four bedrooms of the original house have now been reduced to three. Each room is walled with tongue-and-groove wooden planks, and the beds are built in above storage areas so they are quite high off the ground and resemble ships' bunks.**

THIS PAGE **Philip Hooper journeys all over the world and is quite unable to resist the shells and driftwood he finds on his travels. These are used to create the seaside garden, which is planted with spiky Mediterranean plants. Privacy is preserved because passers-by tend to look at the cactuses first and miss what's afoot in the kitchen.**

THIS PAGE AND OPPOSITE A designer of shops and hotels, David Davies uses his beachside house near Bexhill in England to 'detox' from a busy London life. The Lutyens-esque house is meant to be as relaxing as can be (even though there is an embarrassment of ropes, driftwood and nauticalia). His intention is to keep the colours to a sea-washed minimum – walls, woodwork and floors are all pale – so that attention is always drawn to the views beyond. Many of the lights are made of sea-bleached driftwood and old rope.

huge skies and a world of white

Whiteness, brightness and simplicity are the distinguishing features of this restored 1920s beachside house in the south of England.

You would not think of Sir Edwin Lutyens and the other Edwardian architects who followed in his robust style as being particularly aware of water. Yet, when I recall his conversion of Lindisfarne Castle in Northumberland and his creation of Castle Drogo in Devon, I see that Lutyens's combination of vernacular English detailing and characteristically massive treatment of stout walls – heavy architectural features executed in quality materials throughout – works especially well at the waterside. Inside his houses you feel comfortably protected from the elements, while his gardens, once worked by Gertrude Jekyll, add formality and a sense of place.

David Davies's weekend retreat – he lives by the Thames in Rotherhithe during the week – is a splendid post-Lutyens building of bay windows, dormers and high chimneys dating from the 1920s. It sits, with tremendous presence, just behind the sea wall near Bexhill in Sussex. Between it and the pebbled beach is a formal garden of the Gertrude Jekyll type, which has been recreated by an influential English garden designer, Stephen Woodhams.

The house has been updated by Davies himself, a well-known designer of shops and hotels but never – he laughs – houses. He wants to keep it that way because the house is a retreat from work. 'It's like The Priory to me, a detox centre

from work. My friends all come here to detox from work too because it's so relaxing. In London I can feel exhausted but not here – perhaps because there's nowhere to go.'

One thing that prompted Davies to buy was that he often wanted to be near his parents. 'I had known the house for years, then my sister told me it was for sale. I bought at the very end of the last recession, six years ago. Otherwise I wouldn't have been able to afford it. It was a wreck. Although I'm originally from west London, my parents retired to Sussex, and I used to drive past this house on my way to see them – and dream about living in it. I couldn't believe it when it came on the market. I bought it straight away, but some people thought I was mad.

'The previous occupants had utterly confused the interior by mixing busy wallpaper with deep-pile carpet. It was revolting – the whole place was like a 1950s box from hell. But I could see through that. It is a beautiful house really, and well planned. The true fabric of the building was pretty much untouched. I just had to take it back to its bare bones and start again.'

When he took up the carpets he found the original high-quality wooden floorboards that were a feature of the period. Then he painted everything else white – apart from the original panelling and beams in the hall, living room and dining room. Not only the walls but also the window frames, ceilings, doors, shelves, furniture and light

fittings are painted white. 'My house in London is all white too. I would love to have the gall to paint all the beams white, but I haven't yet. I used lots of different whites – Papers and Paints in London is particularly good on them.'

Where Bexhill has the advantage over London is with the wonderful light that comes from the huge skies and the sea below. Anyone who lives with water knows that each enhances the other: the sky brightens the sea, and the sea reflects more light back to the sky. 'I love the light and the patterns light casts,' says Davies. 'It's ironic that I use colour all the time in my job but can't cope with it away from work. I love the purity of white and, because of the Arts and Crafts influence, and being by the beach, I've used that along with woody textures and tones.' One of the

first changes he made was to double-glaze the windows. The original 1920s windows were rotten and had to be replaced with new ones made to withstand the gale-force winds that are common by the sea. I spoke to him shortly after the worst storms for a decade had ravaged the coast and caused flooding of the small market towns inland. 'The rain was horizontal and I could feel the whole house moving in the wind.'

Curiously, the front of the house faces inland, towards a golf course, but the design is such that it doesn't matter. 'It's very well designed. The front has all the corridors, and the kitchen is at the front too. The back is all windows looking out over the sea. It's absolutely on the beach – the surf crashes at the end. The drawing room

OPPOSITE PAGE AND ABOVE **The Edwardian house has mullioned windows, whose frames Davies has painted matt white. Beside them are white upholstered day beds, white decoy birds and, on the mantelpiece, groups of exotic patterned shells from all over the world.**

BELOW **This stretch of the southern English coastline has long been subjected to erosion from the sea. The south-facing windows provide long views of the 19th-century wooden groynes that were put in place to protect the shore from the encroaching waves.**

THIS PAGE Davies often takes his holidays on the island of Sardinia, and it was there that he found the extraordinary dried twigs that sit in a shell-hung vase.

OPPOSITE PAGE Other drought-loving plants such as spiky aloes are put in white pots in front of the living-room fireplace to combine with furniture all covered in white and with dark wooden ceiling beams and floors. The beach is a constant source of surprises, from sand-eel casts that appear as the tide goes down to seawashed glass and pebbles caught against the retaining groynes.

'I love the light and the patterns light casts. I use colour all the time in my job but dislike it at home. I love the purity of white and, because of the Arts and Crafts influence, and being by the beach, I've used that along with woody textures and tones.'

has bay windows looking out at the sea and there's a conservatory that's basically a glassed-in verandah. It's a marvellous space all year round and everyone spends all their time in there.'

The décor of the house is inspired by the light, the sea and the shingle beach, which has heavy wooden groynes marching far out into the water, built to protect the coast from erosion. The rooms are full of bits of worn driftwood and sea-washed ropes found among the shingle; there are decoy ducks, shells and sea-smoothed pebbles. Paintings – propped rather than hung, to preserve the essential whiteness – refer to yachts and lighthouses, brilliant blue coastal skies and bright sands. Many of the objects are presents from friends who can't resist the ambience. 'Pebbles and shells work naturally down here – but I must try not to buy any more lifebuoys and fishing nets. I've got to be careful not to go over the top with it all. It's a fine balance between the tasteful and kitsch.'

Sardinia is a favourite holiday spot. 'I love it and go there for two weeks every year, staying in the same house.' From the island come shells and twigs. Two particularly clever wall lamps made of

THE DECOR IS INSPIRED BY THE LIGHT, THE SEA AND THE SHINGLE BEACH. THE ROOMS ARE FULL OF BITS OF WORN DRIFTWOOD AND SEA-WASHED ROPES FOUND AMONG THE SHINGLE; THERE ARE DECOY DUCKS, SHELLS AND SEA-SMOOTHED PEBBLES. PAINTINGS – PROPPED RATHER THAN HUNG, TO PRESERVE THE ESSENTIAL WHITENESS – REFER TO YACHTS AND LIGHTHOUSES, BRILLIANT BLUE COASTAL SKIES AND BRIGHT SANDS.

spiky twigs (with electric wiring concealed in the centre of the wood) are from the island, as is the clump of bleached and twisted dried stems that sits in a shell-hung pot – a white pot, of course. 'The house lends itself to these bleached colours, to glass and steel. I find it incredibly pleasing – perhaps because I don't like things engineered and polished.'

Although they are not obvious, Davies made quite a few economies in the house. A hideous 'pebble-dashed' fireplace was entirely plastered over and painted white. The kitchen, facing the golf course, was made from Ikea units. Then Davies found that the heavy wooden beams were, in fact, made of polystyrene, so they had to go, while the whole was given a Portland stone floor. To the outrage of some conservationists, he also took out the original bathroom and put in 'a very nice, very simple' alternative.

Indeed, simplicity is everything here, with the décor being subordinated to the view and the sea. 'I believe buildings have karma built into them for good or bad. This is a very, very happy place. Waking up is amazing. The birds make it an ornithologist's dream, and the marshes nearby are a sanctuary for birds. The sounds they make are fascinating. Inland, nature tends to be concealed, but here it is always interesting, an experience. When it's hot, it's baking; when it's windy, it's really windy. I can't believe how harsh the winters can be – sometimes the plants in the garden are blown at 45 degrees and look quite dead. Then it all comes back in the spring.'

The planting is mostly of those Mediterranean species that can cope with wind, drought, salty air and sharp drainage. Rosemary, santolina, sage, some lavender, cardoons – 'I just love them' – and tamarisk which, despite its delicate appearance, survives the storms.

Stephen Woodhams did little to change the overall formal design, 'though he did increase the size of the beds – they were rather mean'. But he imported quantities of seawashed pebbles, which alternate with the low plantings of santolina and purple sage in the beds – all protected from the elements by low woven-willow hurdles. Large terracotta pots with symmetrical box bushes lead the eye past a central urn loaded with circular stones down to the stony beach itself. Seen from the upstairs windows, this formal arrangement with massive vernacular touches makes the perfect transition from the solidity of the house to the wilderness of the beach beyond.

THIS PAGE AND OPPOSITE
David Davies tries to keep the quantities of nauticalia that silt up his house under control – but it's a battle. Pond yachts, twiggy lights found in Sardinia, models and drawings of lighthouses, and balls of grainy stone keep turning up. He does his best. Only a few are allowed on the all-white shelves and glass-topped tables, in order to preserve the sense that this coastal house is flooded with light.

The Bajan architect Larry Warren is enormously influential in Barbados, where he has his practice. Unlike so many of his peers, who are determined to break with the past, he derives huge inspiration from the traditional styles of vernacular buildings – that is, those done by the local people, often without the involvement of an architect – and is determined to retain the island's very own sense of style and design.

Colonial architecture evolved here and elsewhere in the West Indies when the English first arrived in the 17th century, originally as pioneers but with well-established views about the way in which houses should be built. As the decades progressed and turned into the 18th and 19th centuries, the island became permanently settled by planters, who ran their sugar plantations and molasses and rum factories. Sugar cane was heavily planted, and the products that were made from it became the main export back to Europe. Barbados was the planters' home.

They and their families gradually became rich and influential, and with increasing prosperity came the desire to import to the island the elegant fashions which were sweeping Britain: the Italianate Palladian architecture with its strict rules of proportion, the latest invention of sash windows with good-sized panes of glass, and the furniture that drew inspiration from classical Greece and Rome. Some of the discipline got lost the process but, more

THIS PAGE AND OPPOSITE
The beachside complex of Waverley originally consisted of three Victorian town houses. These have been converted into a holiday residence by Larry Warren, an architect renowned for his imaginative adaptation of

18th-century vernacular island architecture. From the sheltered area beside the pool a path leads directly to the beach. Heavy-leafed bananas lean over the shaded bar with its ugly – though no doubt comfy – white cane chairs.

elegance in the colonial style

The inspiration is the traditional vernacular style of the Caribbean island – that is, buildings built by local people, often without the involvement of an architect.

THIS PAGE AND OPPOSITE
Large French windows allow the trade winds to flow through the main living area with its shell-upholstered chairs and stools. To the left there is also a dining room. All the walls and floors are in the local cream coral stone, and the furniture is chosen to mingle with its colours – and for its coolness. Navy cushions, so neatly arranged on their corners, will soon get ruffled and disorganized when the guests arrive.

importantly, something more was added. The settlers found that the Georgian architecture which was fine in Bath and Boston was not so good in the heat and humidity of Bridgetown, so they started also borrowing from the Mediterranean notions of the French who, along with the Spanish and the Portuguese, had colonized other Caribbean islands.

From the Mediterranean came jalousies – louvred shutters that kept out the glare of the sun while allowing any little breeze to filter indoors – along with cold stone floors, corridors open from front to back to catch the winds, and an overall preponderance of white on the walls, floors, ceilings, fabrics and paintwork. Heavily shaded verandahs, with more louvred shutters, came, as the name 'verandah' suggests, from another British colony, India.

It is this amalgamation of styles, which became characteristic of the Caribbean as a whole, that Larry Warren has captured so well. He uses it both when restoring old buildings and when creating new houses for the fortunate people who can afford holiday homes on the island. Warren generally searches out those old houses that need his touch – he is clearly determined to save what he can of the historic architecture – and, as a result, owns a couple himself.

One of Warren's properties, the Victorian conglomeration of Waverley, has been transformed into a holiday home for visitors to Barbados. 'It consists of three town houses in the centre of Gibbs Bay, maybe the most desirable after the famous Sandy Lane,' he says. 'The town houses take their name from the original seaside residence that occupied the site.

'The architecture is a blend of modern and the traditional stone architecture of the Barbadian residences of the Victorian era, which evolved from the wooden chattel house. Regrettably, these architectural gems are disappearing all too quickly from Barbados's roadside scene.'

THIS PAGE **The guest
bedroom, like many in these
parts, has been designed
to have its own balcony
overlooking the sea. White
louvred blinds and a latticed
bedhead are combined with
stark white walls to give a
deliciously cool impression.**

OPPOSITE PAGE **The guest
balcony follows through
on the white theme, with
white trellis arching over the
verandah, white rush chairs
set around a simple wooden
table, and slanting louvres
to take advantage of the
trade winds. Beyond is a
lush tropical garden.**

Waverley, as recreated by Warren, is a series of cool white rooms, some indoors, some on shaded verandahs, some outside where huge leafy palms and banana trees provide both shadow and splashes of emerald green against the neutrals of faded wood and coral stone.

Even though space was tight, Warren was determined to give the houses vibrant tropical gardens. 'I put great emphasis on creating a private garden between the residence and the beach, with dense planting dividing the spaces. This has given a pleasant shaded outdoor space for residents and their children, who can safely play in the garden area.' His own home, Wyndover, is also notable for its lush gardens as well as horse paddocks amid 6 acres of land that includes a deep ravine. 'As an architect looking for a "new" home, I was determined to find an existing residence to renovate – I would for ever be redesigning a new home, always wondering whether it could have been done differently.

'Wyndover was perfect. Over the years it had been renovated, well built with good and bad features. But the striking aspect of this residence was its simple West Indian appearance, large verandahs and many opportunities for outdoor living.' While Warren focused on the garden at his own home, Waverley is directed towards the beach. From the main living space, which includes both dining and sitting rooms, there is a cool covered and paved area which gives directly onto the blue waters of the pool with its bar and barbecue.

From this water it is only a short walk along a path to the beach itself which, like many on Barbados, is a vision of white sand, soothing palm trees and invitingly deep-blue clear water. 'As with most upmarket property along the west coast of the island, frontage is limited, so it was quite an exercise to provide three

FROM THE MEDITERRANEAN CAME LOUVRED SHUTTERS TO KEEP OUT THE GLARE OF THE SUN WHILE ALLOWING ANY LITTLE BREEZE TO FILTER INDOORS, ALONG WITH COLD STONE FLOORS, CORRIDORS OPEN TO CATCH THE WIND AND A PREPONDERANCE OF WHITE

bedrooms and two bathrooms along with a small plunge pool and spacious living areas – all within a 22 foot frontage. The interior is a blend of coral stone walls, plaster floors and bleached pine and local carved stone, with a collection of paintings by local artists. All this, we hope, contributes to a Barbados experience for the guests.'

Larry Warren's wife, Anna, designed the inside of Waverley. 'The interiors reflect a collection of my wife's taste and our lifestyle. The residence takes its style from Barbados and is not pretentious but simple and to the point.

'The main living area is a large verandah surrounding an outdoor coral-stone room facing west to the sea, which remains untouched by the easterly trade winds. This exposure is ideal since the winds are always available but the rains are never an intrusion.

The large formal dining room is for special occasions, but it also serves as a room where Anna is able to display some of her collections of furniture and accessories. Anna has very good taste – at least, I think so.'

That is evident from her calm interiors at Waverley. Virtually everything is white, but a clever and sophisticated series of different shades of white. Outdoor doors and shutters look antique and distressed, their old white paint just slightly lighter than the beautiful soft creams of the coral stone. Woodwork, such as the lattice work around the plain stone verandah pillars and the louvred jalousies which keep the sun from the outdoor rooms, is softly grey. Mirror frames are brushed with white, and white tiles line the white bath, with white fluffy towels slung over a white bathrail.

Occasionally white gives way to a cool blue, as in the main living room, where the comfy wicker chairs have cushions upholstered in a fabric scattered with blue tropical shells, and the cushions on the dining chairs mirror the blue Bristol glass on the table and the striped rugs on the floor. Shells and fish are a recurrent theme.

It is important when decorating a house for holiday visitors that the local style is used throughout. If you are visiting Barbados, you don't want to feel that the rooms are standardized hotel décor. Waverley certainly avoids the mundane in favour of the old colonial traditions which make so much sense on a tropical island with its drenching storms and debilitating heat.

Larry Warren even has some advice on coping with the indigenous monkeys that can often be seen the trees. 'The house is shared with a troop of monkeys that rarely encroach on our space. The key is never to interact with them – only observe. Like clockwork, they go and return every morning and afternoon, swing from the ample trees until they reach the safety of the gulley.'

Like much of living beside the water, the secret is to sit calmly and at peace, watching the beauties of nature all around.

'The residence takes its style from Barbados and is not pretentious but simple and to the point. The main living area is a large verandah surrounding an outdoor coral stone room facing west to the sea.'

Larry Warren's designs
contrive to develop the
Barbadian vernacular style,
which was inspired by
Georgian Britain, ante-bellum
America, colonial India and
Spain. Jalousies, cool cut
stonework, deep verandahs
and generous windows add
tropical touches to a classical
foundation – all without any
pretentiousness.

picture credits

l = left, **r** = right, **c** = centre

1 Camp Kent designed by Alexandra Champalimaud; **2** Interior Designer Philip Hooper's own house in East Sussex; **3** Elena Colombo's cottage on the east end of Long Island; **4 r** Suzy & Graham Hursts' house in Palm Beach, Sydney, New South Wales; **6** Joan & Ben Francis-Joneses' house in Woy Woy designed by Richard Francis-Jones; **10 r** Camp Kent designed by Alexandra Champalimaud; **13** Suzy & Graham Hursts' house in Palm Beach, Sydney, New South Wales; **26–27** A house in Maine designed by Stephen Blatt Architects; **28 l** Camp Kent designed by Alexandra Champalimaud; **28 r** Compound by a lakeside in the mountains of western Maine designed by Stephen Blatt Architects; **29 l** Fern Mallis's house in Southampton, Long Island; **29 r** A house in Maine designed by Stephen Blatt Architects; **30–39** Fern Mallis's house in Southampton, Long Island; **40–47** Compound by a lakeside in the mountains of western Maine designed by Stephen Blatt Architects; **48–57** Camp Kent designed by Alexandra Champalimaud; **58–63** A house in Maine designed by Stephen Blatt Architects; **66 l** Rupert Morgan's barge in Paris; **66 r** Les Reedman's house on Dangar Island, New South Wales, Australia; **67 cr** Roderick & Gillie Jameses' house in Devon designed by Roderick James Architects and built by Carpenter Oak & Woodland Co. Ltd; **67 r** A houseboat in Paris owned by a nature lover who wants to feel closer to the country; **68–77** Roderick & Gillie Jameses' house in Devon designed by Roderick James Architects and built by Carpenter Oak & Woodland Co. Ltd; **78–83** Terry & Heather Dorroughs' house on Dangar Island, New South Wales designed by Terry Dorrough Architect; **84–87** Peter & Tonia Tesorieros' apartment in Sydney designed by Alexander Tzannes Associates (**84–85** photo by Brian Leonard); **88–93** Les Reedman's house on Dangar Island, New South Wales, Australia; **94–97** Rupert Morgan's barge in Paris; **98–101** A houseboat in Paris owned by a nature lover who wants to feel closer to the country; **102–103** Laurence & Yves Sabourets' house in Brittany; **104 cl** & **cr** Alan & Diana Cardys' house in Sydney designed by The Cox Group; **104 r** The Gardenia residence, Barbados, designed by Larry Warren; **105 l, cl** & **r** A house in Cape Elizabeth designed by Stephen Blatt Architects; **105 cr** Philip Cox's house in Palm Beach designed by The Cox Group; **106–109** Robert & Gabrielle Reeveses' house in Clareville designed by Stutchbury & Pape Architecture + Landscape Architecture; **110–15** Philip Cox's house in Palm Beach designed by The Cox Group; **116–25** Laurence & Yves Sabourets' house in Brittany; **126–33** A house in Cape Elizabeth designed by Stephen Blatt Architects; **134–39** The Gardenia residence, Barbados, designed by Larry Warren; **142 l** Elena Colombo's cottage on the east end of Long Island; **142 r** Waverley townhouse, Barbados, designed by Larry Warren; **143 r** Interior Designer Philip Hooper's own house in East Sussex; **144–53** Elena Colombo's cottage on the east end of Long Island; **154–59** Four Winds, Barbados, designed by Larry Warren; **160–69** Interior Designer Philip Hooper's own house in East Sussex; **170–77** David Davies's house in East Sussex, England; **178–85** Waverley townhouse, Barbados, designed by Larry Warren.

The author and publisher would like to thank the people listed above for providing photographic locations.

architects & designers whose work is featured in this book

Stephen Blatt Architects

10 Danforth Street
Portland
Maine 04101
USA
t. +1 207 761 5911
f. +1 207 761 2105
e. sba@sbarchitects.com
Architectural design firm.
Pages **26–27**, **28 r**, **29 r**, **40–47**, **58–63**, **105 l, cl** & **r**, **126–33**

Alexandra Champalimaud & Associates Inc.

One Union Square West, # 3
New York
NY 10003
USA
t. +1 212 807 8869
f. +1 212 807 1742
www.acainteriordesign.com
Interior architecture and design.
Pages **1**, **10 r**, **28 l**, **48–57**

Terry Dorrough Architect

14 Riverview Avenue
Dangar Island
NSW 2083
Australia
t. +61 2 9985 7729
f. +61 2 9985 7177
Design of houses and small projects.
Pages **78–83**

Carpenter Oak & Woodland Co. Ltd

Hall Farm
Thickwood Lane
Colerne
Chippenham
Wiltshire SN14 8BE
t. 01225 743089
Specialists in the construction of new oak-framed buildings and timber engineering.
Pages **66cr**, **68–77**

The Cox Group

204 Clarence Street
Sydney 2000
Australia
t. +61 2 9267 9599
f. +61 2 9264 5844
e. sydney@cox.com.au
www.cox.com.au
Architects and planners.
Pages **104 cl** & **cr**, **105 cr**, **110–15**

Richard Francis-Jones MGT Architects

Level 4, 261 George Street
Sydney
NSW 2000
Australia
t. +61 2 9251 7077
f. +61 2 9251 7072
e. richard.francis-jones @sydney.mgtarchitects.com
Multi-award-winning architects who have recently received Australia's highest award for excellence in the design of public buildings; they also undertake many residential projects.
Page **6**

Philip Hooper

Studio 30

The Old Latchmere School

38 Burns Road

London SW11 5GY

t. 020 7978 6662

f. 020 7223 3713

Interior designer.

Pages **2**, **142 r**, **160–69**

Les Reedman

P.O. Box 148

Brooklyn

NSW 2083

Australia

t. +61 2 9985 7893

f. (Brooklyn P.O.) +61 2 9985 7658

Chartered architect and

architectural historian.

Pages **66 r**, **88–93**

Alexander Tzannes Associates
Pty Limited

63 Myrtle Street

Chippendale

NSW 2008

Australia

t. +61 2 9319 3744

f. +61 2 9696 1170

e. tzannes@tzannes.com.au

Architecture, interior design.

Pages **84–87**

Roderick James Architects

Seagull House

Dittisham Mill Creek

Dartmouth

Devon TQ6 0HZ

t. 01803 722474

An architectural practice specializing

in contemporary wood and glass

buildings.

Pages **66 cr**, **68–77**

Stutchbury & Pape Architecture +
Landscape Architecture

4/364 Barrenjoey Road

Newport

NSW 2106

Australia

t. +61 2 9979 5030

f. +61 2 9979 5367

e. snpala@ozemail.com.au

Have a reputation for innovative

thinking and environmental

sensitivity. The land, site and place

are seen as directives toward the

solution of formulating a building.

Pages **106–109**

Larry Warren Architect

Derricks

St James

Barbados

t. +1 246 432 6392/2409

f. +1 246 432 2976

Pages **104 r**, **134–39**, **142 r**,

154–59, **178–85**

index

Page numbers in italics denote
captions/illustrations only.